Confessions of a Paris Party Girl

A HUMOROUS TRAVEL MEMOIR

VICKI LESAGE

press

Published by Party Girl Press

ISBN-13: 978-1494701529
ISBN-10: 1494701529

Cover design by Ellen Meyer and Clara Vidal
Author photo by Mickaël Lesage and Damien Croisot

CATCH UP ON THE

American in Paris

BEST-SELLING SERIES

Find out about new releases and deals
by signing up for Vicki's newsletter:
https://bit.ly/lesage-news

(She'll even send you *Confessions & Cocktails* for free!)

For Mika, who helps me survive France

Prologue

Confessions at the Departure Gate

"Last call for flight 815 to Paris. Dernier appel pour le vol 815 à destination de Paris."

I sized up the line snaking around the check-in counter. I had a few more minutes to scribble some notes in my journal.

I've never understood the appeal of French guys. From what I've seen, they're mostly wimpy wienies.

As much of a math nerd as I am, I simply cannot tell time the European way. I may have aced Differential Equations in college but 20:10 will always seem like 10:10 pm to me.

I love Brie and Camembert and Roquefort and Cantal. But there's a special place in my heart for the unnatural orange hue of Kraft Macaroni and Cheese.

And yet, here I was, bags packed, apartment sublet, and on my way to Paris. What was I getting myself into?

1

Sister Mary Keyholder

I would like to say that when I first stepped off the plane and embarked on my new life in France, something memorable happened. Or something funny or amazing or romantic or at least worth writing about. Truth is, I don't remember. I take that to be a good thing. Considering all the mishaps I've had since moving here, "uneventful" nearly equals "good" in my book.

Looking back all these years later, I see myself as a hopeful, naive girl full of energy stepping off that plane. Tired of running into my ex-boyfriend seemingly everywhere around my midwestern American hometown, and having been unceremoniously freed from my IT job, this fearless 25-year-old was ready for a change.

I had dipped my toes in the proverbial European pond over the course of several college backpacking trips and now wanted to experience living there. To wake up to the smell of fresh croissants, to drink copious amounts of wine straight from the source, and maybe meet a tall, dark and handsome Frenchman. Who was, of course, not a wienie.

Oh, to be back in the shoes (or flip-flops, as it were) of that intrepid girl, arriving in a new land, successfully commandeering the Métro and her luggage, triumphantly arriving on the doorstep of her destination.

The smooth sailing didn't last long.

I had sublet an apartment for the summer from an unseen Irish girl, Colleen, using Craigslist. The photos showed a charming, yet tiny, apartment that I already pictured myself living in. You'd think this was where the story starts to go wrong, but the girl and the apartment did exist! Making it probably the last apartment to be legitimately rented online before scammers cornered the market.

For me, the issue was getting *in* to the apartment.

First I had to get the key. Colleen had agreed to leave it next door at the convent (Me? Living next to a convent? This'll be good.) The Catholic schoolgirl in me had an overly romanticized notion of how a Parisian convent would look. I was expecting some sort of Gothic cathedral with nunny looking nuns. So I must have walked past the modern, imposing structure about twenty times, sure I'd been conned, before I noticed the sign. Ahem.

I retrieved the key using a combination of my shaky French and the logic that, c'mon ladies, how would anyone else have found out about this bizarre scenario and come knocking on your door?

"Bonjour, je m'appelle Vicki. Comment allez-vous?" I asked the group of navy-blue-clad, pious-looking women gathered inside the doorway.

The elderly (aren't they all?) nun closest to me cautiously replied, "Pas mal. Et vous?"

Ack! What did she say? I was so busy forming my question I didn't plan for her response! Just keep going, you can do it. "Je cherche une clef." I'm looking for a key.

"Une clef?"

"Oui, une clef." Now I know that's not much to go on, but let's be real. Do lost girls often come to their door? Hrm. Now that I think about it, maybe that's how girls become nuns? Better speed this up before I get stuck in the nunnery, never to be seen again. "Colleen leave key? It's for me."

"Oh yes, a key! For an American girl. That must be you." Was it that obvious? Was it my blonde hair? Wide, toothy smile? No, it was probably my command (or lack thereof) of the French language.

"You're friends with Colleen?" she asked.

I wasn't sure how to answer that since we weren't really friends, but then again I wasn't even sure that was the question. My French wasn't up to the task of explaining how I knew Colleen, and for sure if I said we *weren't* friends, Sister Mary Keyholder would never hand over the precious key.

"Yes," I said with a smile, then promptly got the heck out of there.

Key and two heavy suitcases in hand, I headed to my new apartment building. The number on the front, 20, was written in the ornate curlicue script that most French buildings employ. The large windows of each apartment were fronted by black wrought-iron rails, providing the perfect vantage point from which to observe the goings-on of the street below. I eagerly punched the five-digit code into the digicode reader to the right of the door and was in.

Next issue: finding the actual apartment. You'd think this would be easy since Colleen had said it was on the third floor. Silly me, that seemed like enough information until I scoped out the situation.

Problem 1: Once inside the front door, I saw two buildings—one that faced the sidewalk (in which I was currently standing) and one past a quiet courtyard containing a few trees and a large, overflowing trash barrel.

Which building was it?

Problem 2: Colleen had said the apartment was on the third floor but in France the ground floor is counted as the "0th" floor, so what an American calls the third floor, a French person calls the second floor. I didn't know if Colleen had adjusted for the American way or stuck to the French method or if Ireland had an entirely different technique.[1]

Problem 3: Each floor had two apartments.

So I had a total of eight possible apartments to choose from, none of which had names on the door. I was afraid to leave my bags unattended so I schlepped up the first set of stairs, bags and all, and knocked on each door. On any door where I didn't get a response, I tried my key. No dice in any of the apartments in the first building, so I hauled my luggage down the stairs and through the courtyard to the second building. One person answered and had no idea who Colleen was (friendly neighbors!) and I tried my key in the other three doors. But again, no dice. Crap! After trying eight different apartments, one of them should have been the right one.

I sulked down to the courtyard and let out a few choice words of frustration. I thought back to when my mom and step-dad, Doug, were seeing me off at the airport. We had

---

[1] I've dedicated many a conversation to this topic because that's the kind of life I lead (if you understand that, you're going to *love* this book) and I still can't tell which system is better. I can see counting the ground floor as the first floor because it has a floor and it's the first one you walk on. But I can also see the logic in going up your first flight of stairs and then counting "1", then another flight and saying "2" and so on. I mean, are you trying to get credit for making it to the ground floor when you haven't even gone anywhere? When you're not in a building do you say you're on the first floor? No, because you're just on the ground! So I guess we'll have to call it a wash. Sit back and relax—I'll take care of sending the memo to America and France so they know what I've decided on this important matter. And I still don't know how they do it in Ireland!

a tearful goodbye and I choked up when my mom said "Good luck in your new life, honey." She was sad to see me go but wanted me to be happy. And now here I was, trapped outside my new apartment, admittedly not doing so hot in this new life.

I wanted to call her and cry but I needed to get into the apartment to get the damn phone! Plus, I didn't want to give Mom a heart attack by waking her at 5:00 in the morning. No, better to sort everything out myself and call when I had good news to report.

I straightened up and reassessed the situation. I know I'm at the right address since the front door code worked. Colleen hadn't said anything about crossing the courtyard, so her apartment is probably in the first building. And since we're in France, she had probably used the French system of floor numbering.

Not giving a rat's ass about the suitcases anymore, and hating their guts for being so stubbornly heavy, I hauled my sweaty self up the first stairs once again and tried both apartments on the (French) third floor.

Funny thing, no matter how determined you are, if the key ain't right for the door, it ain't gonna open. And this key was a monster. At least twice as large as a standard door key, it squirmed of its own volition, so determined was it to *not* fit in the door.

Now I was dejected. I went back to the sunny courtyard to throw insults at my luggage and half-seriously glanced around for a place to sleep. Behind the trash bin? Under the tree? Maybe with enough *vin rouge* I could make the courtyard comfortable. I turned to the sky for answers (why do people do that?) and that's when I noticed the burgundy curtains in an apartment on the third floor of the second building. I recognized the color from one of the Craigslist ad photos. At last! This could be it. So looking at the sky *does* provide answers.

Leaving the luggage once again, I climbed the stairs and

tried the key in the door. It wasn't easy going, but I was more determined than ever. I shimmied and I shook. This key had to fit! I was NOT sleeping under a tree!

With vigorous jiggling, cursing, and promising my firstborn child, the door finally opened. I'd never been more proud of myself in my life. I might have even literally leapt for joy. "Hello, Paris! Vicki is here and watch out, she can OPEN DOORS!"

After touring my new digs, I mustered up the strength to retrieve my luggage. Me! And my bags! In my apartment! With a key that opens doors! Wheee! The possibilities in this new life are endless. If I can open a door, I can do anything!

2

Yes, We Reluctantly Accept Credit Cards

Having expended an absurd amount of energy just getting into my apartment, I was famished. Lucky for me, I was now living in one of the greatest food capitals of the world. I grabbed my wallet and monstrous key and headed down to the local *épicerie*.

This moment right here—walking a few doors down the street to buy food—was one of the main reasons I moved to Paris. I already felt so local. New Yorkers do it all the time but in St. Louis we drive everywhere. We circle around the strip mall parking lot for hours to find the perfect spot, and when we're done with one store we re-park the car if we need to go to a store further down the strip. Then we exit our cars with the telltale smirk of having snagged a great parking spot as we walk the three feet (that's one meter to the rest of the world) to the store. Ah, the good life.

During my backpacking trips across Europe, my

stomach fluttered every time I walked to pick up a baguette. Such a mundane task made me so happy I wanted to do it every day. At some point in my life I just *had* to live in Europe.

I'd studied French in school, though my ability to actually use the language was laughable. When deciding which European country to move to, I thought it would be cool to move to a non-English-speaking country, but felt I was way too old to learn a new language (I was 25, after all).

So that narrowed my choices down to French-speaking countries. I slightly preferred Belgium, where fries, waffles, chocolate, and beer were the major food groups, but was open to France as well. In the end, it boiled down to which place would be easier for me to plan from abroad, and at the time the only French-speaking city that had a Craigslist was Paris.

Go figure. My entire future was based on the accessibility of one website.

Had I done this only a few years later, I might have ended up in an entirely different city. And probably 20 pounds heavier. My jeans were snug as it is (I've been told I have a "butt for jeans," which I think is supposed to be a compliment) and I certainly didn't need any help.

Now happily planted in the City of Light, I was ecstatic to be bounding down the street to the local grocery store. It's the simple pleasures in life, right?

Once inside, the cool air provided a welcome relief from the sweltering summer heat. And what a delight to have so many delicacies right at my fingertips! Ripe cheeses I didn't even know the names of overflowed their lightly refrigerated shelves, while row after row of Bordeaux's tastiest bottles waited to be uncorked and savored. It's like the store could see directly into my brain and stocked up on everything I had fantasized about on my flight across the ocean.

Surreptitiously wiping the drool from my lower lip, I selected some thinly sliced *saucisson,* a round of camembert, and a bottle of red wine. A similar array back home would have set me back an easy $20, likely more. But my basket rang up to 8€, which at the time was about $11. Not too shabby.

"Le minimum pour la carte bleue est 15€," the cashier said, while pointing to a sign I hadn't noticed. The minimum amount to use a credit card was 15 euros.

Coming from a land where you can charge a pack of gum to your card, I was flabbergasted. My 8€ total seemed completely reasonable for a credit card purchase. And since I hadn't yet made it to an ATM, cash wasn't an option. Were they really telling me they'd rather I set my stuff down and walk out the door than accept my credit card?

ৡৡঌ

Looking back on this scene now, I hardly bat an eye. I'm so accustomed to such situations that I always make sure to either have cash on hand or make a hefty minimum purchase. Gone is my arrogance that I should teach "these people" there's an easier way. These are "my people" now and I've learned to accept the nuances of my adopted country, even if it means developing an entirely new (and somewhat ridiculous, to the foreign eye) way of doing things.

Many aspects of shopping have become habit now. If a grocery store closes at 9:45 pm and it's only 9:30, even if I only need to dash in for a carton of milk, I sigh and say "Tomorrow's another day." Because if the store closes at 9:45, those employees will march out of that door at 9:46 so help them God! Their shift is over and they are outta there! Which means that even if you can squeeze past the imposing security guard, who usually blocks entry to this secured fortress as of 9:25, you'll be met with a long line at the only remaining open cashier. You'll panic, wondering if the cashier will take pity on you when you eventually reach her or if she'll close up shop, leaving you milk-less for another day.

Better not to even try. Go back tomorrow and shop in peace.

So you wake up the next day, brew some coffee and plan out the day. You're invigorated by the caffeine but you're careful not to let your buzz trick you into something foolish. You set the bar low with a simple declaration of "I'm gonna get that milk I dreamed about yesterday. Oh, and I'll pick up some cash at the bank on the way."

You stroll down the quaint street and marvel at how you're able to walk to the bank and the grocery store on the same trip. City living at its finest! You people-watch and absorb the beautiful surroundings.

You saunter up to the ATM, pop in your card, and select the amount of 50€ to withdraw, thinking this is a happy medium between carrying around a large wad of cash and having to go to the ATM every day. Out pops a huge 50-euro note, which you swiftly stuff into your too-small American wallet before resuming your jaunty stroll. Life is good.

You enter the store well within opening hours, grab a carton of unrefrigerated milk (by now you've gotten used to the concept of buying room-temperature milk), pick up a few other items, and head to the cash register.

Then, because you're a jerk, you try to pay for a 10€ purchase with a fifty.

"Who are you, Satan's spawn? Why would you do such an abhorrent thing?" The cashier might not say it out loud, but you can tell by her face that these words are crossing her mind. It's as if she's going to have to break that fifty out of her own money and the store won't even reimburse her. Her kids will starve and drop out of school and it's all your fault.

I'm always surprised by their expression of sheer horror when you hand them a fifty. I mean, it can't be the first time they've seen one. And surely they have change in their till. Or do they start at zero each day and hope that everyone pays in exact change until enough of a stash is built up? If so, they should at least have a sign that says "We don't accept fifties until after lunch, you crazy fools."

"Avez-vous un billet plus petit?"

They always ask if you have a smaller bill. If I had a smaller bill, I would have offered it in the first place. I'm trying to make this transaction as short as possible. But even after you politely apologize for not having a lower denomination (because clearly this is a situation where *you* should be apologizing) there's still the requisite 5-second pause where they stare you down and see if you'll cave in. Even if I did have something smaller, I'm not admitting it now! But trust me, I don't have a smaller bill because every other store rejected my fifty, too.

"Non, j'ai juste ma carte bleue."

Offering to pay by credit card offends them even more deeply to their already deeply offended core. It's a good way to show that making change for your fifty is the lesser of the two evils.

Eventually, after they feel you've suffered enough, they'll begrudgingly accept your fifty-euro note. This arduous task is usually accompanied by a medley of sighs and groans, peppered with a few eyebrow-raises and head-shakes. Once you've been sufficiently shamed, you will receive your change, which is always handed to you bills first, then coins on top, so that the coins spill all over the place and make you look like an incompetent jerk who's holding up the line (which, unfortunately at this point, you are).

૭∾ર

These days, you won't catch me in that situation. I have a meticulous plan to avoid all that:

1. Only withdraw 40€ at a time from the cash point. Sure, you'll be making more visits to the ATM, but at least you'll never be burdened with a fifty. Or if you want to get fancy, conduct two transactions of 40€ withdrawals in a row. Yes, you are wasting valuable time that could be spent enjoying Parisian life, but you'll be the proud owner of four 20€ notes, and that's priceless.

2. If burdened with bills even as offensive as a twenty, load up your basket and get that purchase amount as close to twenty euros as you can without going over. All those years of watching The Price is Right have paid off. You can always fit in another bottle of wine.

3. Shoot for a minimum purchase of 15€. Even if you just stopped in for some juice, throw in a bottle of Bailey's to hit your credit card minimum. Yes, it's 10:30 in the morning but you'll get fewer dirty looks this way.

4. If you do ever get stuck with a fifty, hold your ground when using it. Maintain eye contact with a look that says "I may have two perfectly fine tens in my wallet but when I woke up this morning I set out to get rid of my fifty and that means you're the unlucky recipient. If you think THIS is bad, you don't even want to know what else I'm capable of."

It's quite simple, actually. I'll wait while you print this for future reference.

Too bad I didn't have these years of wisdom during that first fateful trip to the grocery store. Since creating a scene isn't my style—I much prefer to snark about it later or write an entire book about it—I snatched up my products and returned to the aisles, hurriedly scanning for anything to bulk up my purchase.

The store had taken on a different look. The cheese stank and the bottles of wine were boringly similar. Slow-moving grannies blocked every aisle. The store that had minutes before been a dreamland was now coming into sharp focus—and it wasn't pretty.

I panicked.

I needed to get that total up to 15€ and fast because the growling of my stomach was now audible. In a desperate move lacking inspiration, I simply retraced my steps and bought two of everything I'd originally picked up.

Relieved, I made my way back to the cashier, paid with my credit card, and was on my slightly-less-merry way.

3

Broom vs. Wine, The Eternal Debate

I enjoyed nearly every aspect of my new apartment. The hardwood floors were old and creaky—or in my eyes, authentic and beautiful. The shower didn't have a curtain, which simply provided a better view of the wooden sauna-like walls of the bathroom. The antique sofa was uncomfortable, which ensured I didn't waste time lounging around when I could be exploring Paris.

As the summer sun beat down in the courtyard, the apartment itself stayed impossibly cool. I kept the screenless windows open at all times, and had pulled a rickety table up to the window where I would eat, work on my laptop, and generally think to myself, "This is the life." Before heading overseas, I'd secured a few web design gigs, a great way to earn extra cash while still having time to enjoy my new city.

There are two major drawbacks to having the windows open, though. I discovered the first one day when I had left to run some errands and returned to a big pile of bird crap on my kitchen floor. Thankfully the bird had already flown away but as I scanned the kitchen, I imagined everything its creepy bird claws had touched and germy feathers had brushed against. I'm selectively germaphobic and this scenario was shooting straight off my germ-meter. After removing the poop with a wad of paper towels the size of Massachusetts, I scrubbed down every surface and re-washed any dish that had been exposed.

Then I rewarded myself with a glass of wine and surveyed my domain. The thought briefly crossed my mind that perhaps the bird had not confined itself to the kitchen and had maybe nibbled on my toothbrush or took a nap on my bed. It could have flown in my closet and tried on my clothes or browsed through one of my books while spending some leisurely time on the toilet. No, at least that last part wasn't true since he had clearly taken care of his toilet needs in my kitchen.

Rather than scour every inch of my apartment, which was small but not *that* small, I simply poured another glass of wine. See? Selective germaphobia.

The second drawback to screenless windows is the dust that gathers. You'd think that facing the courtyard as opposed to the street would mean that only beautiful rays of sunshine would work their way in, but somehow the apartment was incredibly dusty all the time. You'd also think that the tenant of such an apartment would have a broom.

To be fair, Colleen had left a miniature hand broom with a correspondingly miniature dust pan. While a 20 square meter apartment is tiny by most standards (that's only about 215 square feet), it becomes quite large when faced with the task of using a hand broom to sweep it.

So I set out in search of a normal, upright broom. Since I was on a budget and every euro spent on purchases like this was one euro less to spend on wine, I was looking for a bargain.

There were no bargains to be had.

See, that's the thing about large cities—they know when they've got you. Unless you want to procure a car and head outside the city to Ikea, you're stuck paying the exorbitant prices that the local stores charge. I suppose it's noble to keep cutesy mom and pop shops in business, but Mom and Pop don't seem so cute once you realize they're ripping you off.

I visited three different stores in my neighborhood. The first had mops and plant pots and dish towels but no brooms. The second had brooms for 30€. The third had brooms for 28€. That hand broom suddenly looked pretty good.

I wandered the store, debating what to do. I passed a 300€ toilet roll holder and did a double-take. The heck? If I had that much money to burn I could hire someone to hand me toilet paper.

And with that I made a decision. I'd sacrifice my back in support of my budget. I would hunch down on the floor several times per week and sweep with the world's tiniest broom. I can't complain—it made my glass of wine taste that much sweeter.

4

Drinking and Swerving

While Parisian grocery stores and wine shops offer a vast selection of bottles to get your buzz on, there are just as many bars and cafés waiting to offer you equally enjoyable vino. Your choice might be limited to simply "red" or "white" and when noting the price—which can be as low as 2€ per glass—an American would be understandably wary of its drinkability.

No need to worry. France has a reputation to uphold and unless you're in a truly crummy establishment (and even then...) you'll get a pretty good glass of wine.

At 2€ a pop, I typically ordered several. Which led to some swervy walks home, but that is yet another reason I moved to Paris—there's no need to drive anywhere.

ومو

Back in St. Louis, I had a car. You had to.

At age 14, I bussed tables at an upscale Italian restaurant so I could save up to buy my first set of wheels at age 16. My car wasn't the coolest but I loved it because it was mine. I had refilled hundreds of bread baskets and cleared thousands of plates in order to pay for this fuel-burning machine. I had earned it.

The car gave me mechanical trouble here and there, but it was nothing the wages from my part-time jobs couldn't cover. During college, a blown gasket cost me my entire summer's earnings from an actuarial internship in Seattle, but that still didn't get me down. However, after the next breakdown (the car, not me—though I was close to a breakdown myself), it was time to part ways. I couldn't work just to keep my car alive—I had European trips to spend my money on!

The same week I sent my car to the junkyard, I had borrowed a friend's car and accidentally broke his sun visor. At least I knew where I could score a cheap replacement.

"I can give you $125, ma'am. You interested?" The dirty guy behind the counter at the junkyard tapped his pen while I contemplated my options. The car would cost way too much to repair and I'd already paid to haul it there. I couldn't afford any other option.

"Yep, sounds good. Thanks. By the way, do you have any sun visors for a '94 Subaru?"

While he checked, I waved a sniffly goodbye to the teal-colored sedan of my teenage years.

He returned with the part and set it on the greasy counter. "That'll be $25. I'll deduct it from your check."

Ouch! A sun visor was worth 1/5th of my entire car? But what choice did I have?

Since I needed transportation for my job (such a vicious circle!), I hastily bought a replacement car. My brother, Stephen, had been trying to unload his hunk of junk Chevy before he left for a 15-month stint in Iraq. For

$600 (or 24 sun visors), I got a beat-up tin can that ended up lasting me a few years, before I sold it to Stephen's friend for $500 (20 sun visors).

Despite its rusty patches and faded interior, there had been nothing seriously wrong with the Chevy. But once I graduated college and had a steady paycheck, I was ready for a new(ish) car. Something that couldn't be counted by sun visors.

I purchased a gently used black Volkswagen Jetta for a steal and cruised around town without risk of leaving a trail of parts in my wake. I drove this car up until I moved to Paris. Sometimes I still miss it. I mean, I don't stare fondly at pictures of it or anything, but that's only because I don't have any pictures of it.

ഇ∞ഉ

While I liked driving, I did not like the ever-present problem of drinking and driving. In case you haven't caught on by now, I love my wine. But St. Louis is a city with sprawling suburbs and you pretty much have to drive everywhere. That means either choosing a designated driver or exercising control and only having one or two drinks. People rarely volunteer for the first and I'm no good at the second. I've never understood people who just go out for one drink. Once I have one drink, I want *all* the drinks. I'd rather have none than only one!

The best way my friends and I found to get around the problem was to go out for a few drinks, then have "after-bars" at home. No scary drinking and driving to deal with, plus it's a lot cheaper. Win-win.

Except for the neighbors. You see, my friends and I are those annoying girls who, after a few drinks, think they can sing and think everyone else wants to hear it.

At the time, that Romanian pop song, "Dragostea Din Tei" (you might know it as the "My-a-hee, My-a-ho" song) was inexplicably popular. I prided myself on knowing all the lyrics and on more than one occasion, actual Romanians verified that I was in fact singing the correct words. Some people are good at sports, I'm good at singing Eastern European pop chart sensations. We all have our talents.

One cool spring night, I was out with my usual gang. Erin, a short Italian-American and a dreamer who continually achieved her dreams, had been my best friend since the first day of college. Holly, despite her exotic good looks, was a sweetheart I'd been friends with since high school. Monica, who we jokingly referred to as the mom of our group even though she was the same age, lived in the apartment building next door and usually joined us later in the evening.

We were on our way back to my place for after-bars, singing along to everyone's favorite Romanian song. I called Monica to let her know we were almost there. Since she lived so close, she didn't need much advance notice to throw on some shoes and head over.

"HEY!" I had to shout to make myself heard over the awesomeness of the song. "WE'RE GONNA BE HOME IN A FEW MINUTES! COME TO MY PLACE FOR DRINKS!"

"I *know* you're almost home, I can hear that stupid song from all the way down the street," Monica replied.

Ahem. Perhaps our sing-a-longs should have been conducted with the car windows closed, but even then, I'm not sure the ears in the neighborhood would have been safe.

Back at my apartment, we headed out to the balcony, martini in one hand, hairbrush in the other, belting out the likes of Janis Joplin.

Before we knew it (so, probably an hour in sober-people time), five cop cars wailed down the street from both directions and screeched to a halt in front of the apartment building.

We surveyed the situation, speculating which white-trash neighbor was getting busted tonight. The neighborhood wasn't bad, per se, but it wasn't the best either so it wasn't uncommon for something to be going down.

The cops jumped from their cars and slammed their doors. This was going to be good.

A young police officer shouted up to our third-floor balcony, "Are you the singing ladies?"

Wait, what? They're here for *us*? Four twenty-something girls holding hairbrush microphones?

"Did this really necessitate a SWAT team?" Monica half-rhetorically asked.

Monica's fiancé was serving in Iraq. She had enormous respect for authority and on any other day would more likely be the one calling the cops, not having the cops called on her. But the "mother" of our group was feeling sassy that night. Must have been the martinis.

We couldn't help ourselves from snickering.

The police officer tried to remain serious and responded, "Ma'am, we've received noise complaints from the neighbors. You're disturbing the peace. I'm going to need you to stop the singing."

Her slurred voice dripped with sarcasm as she replied, "Yessss, sirrrrr. We'll stop the singing. We're sorry for committing such a heinous crime."

Surprised we had complied so quickly, and clearly having expected much worse when being called to our neighborhood, he replied, "Oh, well... OK then. Thank you. You ladies have a nice evening."

Then Monica said, in what she thought was under her breath but it's never as quiet as you think when you've been drinking, "Sure, whatever, we're gonna crank it up as soon as you leave."

One of the other officers shouted, "I heard that!"

Heh. We were in full giggle mode now. Fortunately, the ten cops realized their time could be better used elsewhere and left us crooners alone.

"Thank you for your service and everything you do for our country, officers!" Gotta love the martini-sass. But c'mon, drug deals are happening around the corner and they're sending five squad cars to quell a few girls?[2]

ஒ௸

Nights like that were harmless. But every time you wanted to party, you had to deal with the driving issue. So while some girls pack their bags for Paris with a gleam in their eye and a dream in their heart, I was more focused on finding a place to party without a car. It's not as eloquent but it's my truth.

Stumbling across the ancient cobbled pavement of my Parisian street, digging in the bottom of my ginormous purse for my huge key—these were the hazards I preferred to face after a night out on the town.

ஒ௸

During my first week in Paris, I ventured out to a few local bars. Fun as it was to run up my phone bill talking to my mom, I needed to get out and meet some people.

My neighborhood was in the quiet, residential 15th *arrondissement*, a bit outside the heart of the city's action but still offering a smattering of lively bars and cafés.

One night, I picked a quirky bar with a funky name. The tiny round tables with off-balance stools were part of its charm, but I chose to sit at the zinc-plated bar where I

---

[2] Incidentally, a few months after moving to Paris, I heard about a shoot-out a few doors down from my old apartment in St. Louis. I can only hope our otherwise-pointless episode trained the officers for a quick response time when it was actually needed.

was more likely to strike up a conversation.

After ordering my *verre de vin rouge* from the bartender, I scoped out the situation. French bartenders aren't chatty like American or Irish bartenders, but there are always other customers to talk to.

"Bonsoir," I said to the loner sitting near me. His surprised expression put me off slightly, but I continued. "Tu habites près d'ici?" I didn't care where he lived but it was the only French sentence I had been able to throw together. Great, now he thought I was casing his house.

"Oui..." he warily responded. He rattled off something else I didn't understand, then finished the rest of his *demi* (that's a half pint for those of you who've never heard of anything so petite) in one gulp. His stool screeched loudly as he scooted away from the bar. "Bonne soirée, mademoiselle."

I couldn't very well have a *bonne soirée* now! He'd made me feel like a lecherous creep hitting on people at the bar, when all I'd meant to do was have a friendly chat. He'd been polite about it but I still felt icky.

Knocking back the rest of my drink, I ordered another while I glanced around the bar. I spotted a group of twenty-somethings clustered around some tables. Not yet deterred from meeting people, I brazenly walked over and asked if I could join.

"Bien sûr!" a dark-haired guy with perfect teeth bellowed. This was more like it.

We passed the evening speaking Franglais, with the Frenchies eager to practice their English, me eager to practice my French, and everyone aided by the free-flowing wine.

"Where are you from?" Perfect Teeth asked.

"St. Louis," I replied. I didn't know if I should include the state, but considering the St. Louis metropolitan area has close to three million inhabitants (making it larger than France's second largest city, Lyon, which is closer to two million), I assumed they had heard of it.

"Ah, oui. I know St. Louis. It's in *Louisiane*, non?"

Clearly he *didn't* know St. Louis. "Close," I politely offered, even though it takes at least nine hours to drive to Louisiana from St. Louis. "C'est dans l'état due Missouri."

He frowned, clearly disappointed he hadn't gotten it right. "C'est difficile, there are 50 states to remember!"

"Don't worry, not even every American knows where St. Louis is." Sad, but true.

ço∕ɹ

I repeated my technique the next few nights, checking out a new venue each time. My French was improving and my phone was filling up with numbers. I had vague plans to meet up with everyone at a later date. *Succès!*

However, upon sober review the next day, I realized only the guys were showing any interest. Each night, the girls would slowly trickle out and I'd be left with an eager Frenchman, wooing me with what he thought were romantic sayings. I'd then receive a barrage of text messages, professing more and more strongly his desire to "show a beautiful lady the light and life of Paris." One guy, who groped my butt before I politely but firmly pushed him away, declared, "My hand discovered a land I would love to explore." I don't even want to know the extent of his plans, but suffice it to say I deleted his text message and his phone number.

Maybe I was naive to think that a girl going out to a bar by herself could make new friends, but it should be possible. It's not that I was against the idea of dating a French guy—I was single after all—it's just that I didn't want to pick up guys at bars, particularly not my first week in Paris. I wanted to establish a group of friends and find my footing in the city before finding a guy.

So how do you make friends in a new place? During

my time in Paris, I've met people in all sorts of ways—work, volunteering, connecting with a friend of a friend from back home, and oh yes, going to bars. But in the beginning, I relied on good old Craigslist.

I placed an ad in the Strictly Platonic section stating that I was an American girl in Paris looking for fun people to hang out with. The first day I had nearly 100 replies from French guys offering to show me the romantic side of their city, and maybe a little more.

So I edited the ad to say "Please, only replies for friendship. No French guys promising to show me how romantic Paris can be." The next day, I had nearly 100 replies from French guys telling me I was missing out on the best of what Paris had to offer.

I edited the ad again, this time to say "No, really. I'm posting this in the platonic section because right now I'm just interested in making friends. Are there any girls out there who understand the situation I'm in?"

Lucky for me, a girl named Lisa replied and was sympathetic to my plight. In fact, she was surprised I hadn't received twice as many replies from guys. Like me, she had nothing against French guys but meeting them via an ad where you explicitly said you were just looking for friendship means you're only going to encounter the overly-eager and/or pushy type. No thanks.

Lisa suggested meeting at an English-speaking bar, called the Fifth Bar, to show me another side of Paris. I could hardly wait.

༄

The pub was on the other side of town but I was in the mood to walk. I overestimated how long it would take, and despite the nearly hour-long stroll, I arrived a bit early. I settled in at the bar and ordered a pint. The bartender was a friendly Irish girl with short, stylish hair and a slightly chipped tooth in her genuine smile. I liked her instantly.

"So where you from? America, I guess, yeah?" she inquired with a strong Dublin accent.

"Yep," I eloquently replied.

"And you're in Paris at an English pub."

"Yep."

"How long you been here?"

"A week."

"Ah, that's about right. Surprised it even took you this long. They all come round to the English pubs sooner or later."

That made me feel better. It's not that I had given up on the French scene—I still loved everything the *brasseries* and cafés had to offer—it's just that I wasn't having much luck making friends.

"I'm Vicki. Nice to meet you."

"Yeah, cool. I'm Anne Marie, but my friends call me Ammo."

୨◦୧

Lisa showed up shortly after. With blonde hair and blue eyes, the tall, thin mid-twenties girl standing before me was undoubtedly a knockout. Of course she understood my Craigslist ad—she probably got hit on by every French guy who crossed her path. Her confidence showed in the way she walked. She clearly knew her way around town.

"Hey, I'm Vicki. You must be Lisa?"

"Hi! And you must be the girl buried by replies to your ad." Turning to Anne Marie, she said, "I'll have a pint, please."

As we got to talking, I learned she was a fellow American, hailing from the East Coast. She had graduated from an Ivy League school and was working in a French law firm while waiting to get accepted to law school in the US. She was fluent in French, but preferred to socialize with Anglophones in English-speaking bars.

I was on board.

There's a certain charm in being able to order a coffee in French at your local café. Or when a stranger asks you directions and you actually know how to help. Or mailing a package at La Poste and asking the requisite questions about the cost and estimated delivery date in the native language.

But when you want to unwind over a drink, it's so much easier to do it in English. And to have people not only understand the words you're using but to understand your situation, because as another English-speaker living in Paris, they're in the same boat.

Anglophones in Paris, and I presume the same happens in other cities, instantly bond. You can't exactly complain to a French person about their country but you need an outlet to vent about all the little things. It's nice to be met with an enthusiastic nod instead of a blank stare, indicating that you are not alone.

Lisa and I swapped story after story about craziness we'd encountered so far in Paris. After a few too many drinks at the pub, we bar-hopped to a few other English-speaking locales in the 5th *arrondissement.* Lisa knew the bartenders at every place, not to mention about half the clientele. I was back in my party girl shoes, retracing the exciting steps from my previous vacations in Paris.

"Paris is so beautiful! Everyone is so nice! We can walk everywhere! I just love everything so much!"

OK, so maybe I was drunk. But still. I was having a great time. And I even had a couple of new friends to share it with.

৯৵৶

Digging through my inbox the next day, amidst spam and the daily email from Mom, I found one other promising response to my ad. Katrina was also American and was working in Paris for the summer. We met up for a drink at a French bar and sat on the *terrasse*, drinking sweet rosé wine as the sun set and the air turned cool.

She could have been my twin sister, with her long blonde hair, green eyes, and thin-but-not-skinny frame. An eternal optimist, Katrina didn't share my complaints but she did notice that French girls on the whole weren't interested in making new friends. Having met someone who liked to talk as much as I did, I sensed she'd probably be game for the English-speaking bar scene so that she could actually converse with people.

I was right.

She agreed that the Parisian scene worked well for restaurants, coffee, and the odd museum here and there. But when you really wanted to have fun, particularly of the late-night drinking variety, the Anglophone scene was more our style.

Katrina, Lisa, and I quickly fell into a groove of hitting up the same bars nearly every night. Each bar had its own set of regulars and its own atmosphere. I loved them all.

One of our favorites was The Long Hop. Our shoes stuck to the grimy floors but we always had a seat at the beat-up wooden bar. The place was usually flooded with students, and I was just young enough to be taken for one myself. People, especially those on vacation, were always curious to find out what I was doing in Paris.

"So, are you on vacation, too?" they'd start out.

"No, actually I live here."

"Oh, so you're studying abroad?"

"Me? Ha, no, I'm not quite that young."

Seeing their puzzled expression as to what any other option could be, I'd help them out. "I work here."

"Oh, right. So what do you do?"

"I'm a freelance web designer."

"So do you, like, eat croissants every day and hang out

at the Eiffel Tower all the time?"

Clearly they don't know how many calories are in a croissant. "Ha, I wish. No, I work in the afternoons and then I come to this bar and blow all my money."

"Can I buy you a drink, then?"

I could really get used to this.

৩৵৶

By night, I partied like crazy. By day, I studiously worked and blogged about my summer in Paris. I wanted to have a record of my adventures, in case I ever got old one day and forgot. That day is approaching sooner than I'd like to admit.

In one blog post, I discussed how the various bars on the usual circuit made Bloody Marys. I preferred my drink with a lot of Worcestershire sauce but was too embarrassed to ask because I didn't know how to pronounce the word.

Taking the hint, one of my blog readers left a comment with the username "Wooster" and explained that's how you pronounce it—"wooster." Isn't the internet wonderful?

Armed with this knowledge, I went on a Bloody Mary tour. First stop, The Long Hop. Their take on the Bloody Mary was decent but pricey, so I stuck to wine after that. The tour could continue after my wallet took a short break.

Since the Long Hop was an "early-closing" bar, everyone had to be out by 2 am. While this is a totally reasonable time, we had a few more hours of partying left in us. So we headed up the adjacent hill and down the cobblestoned rue Mouffetard to the Fifth Bar.

Ammo was working, which guaranteed Kylie Minogue would be playing on the stereo. You've never met a bigger Kylie fan than Anne Marie. No, seriously, you haven't. It's kind of her trademark.

I had a friend in college who was a huge Arnold

Schwarzenegger fan. She'd been obsessed with him ever since she was a little girl. She'd seen all his movies uncountable times and could recite nearly every line. But I didn't truly understand the extent of her love for the strong-jawed Austrian star until I visited her house, where several cardboard cutouts lined her living room. When Kindergarten Cop startled me in the bathroom, I knew I had met the Governator's biggest fan.

Accordingly, cardboard cutouts can be used as a gauge of fandom. Anne Marie has a cardboard cutout of Kylie. Now you get the idea?

⚭

Walking up rue Mouffetard, we could hear Kylie from the street.

"Hiya," Ammo greeted as we walked in. "What are you's having?"

Katrina ordered a beer while I ordered a Bloody Mary. "With lots of 'wooster' please."

"Did you say wooster?" a pretty girl, about my age, with reddish brown hair asked. She was sitting at the end of the bar, near the stereo.

"Yep, I did. Because now I know how to say it, thanks to someone who commented on my blog."

Before I had a chance to explain, since that sentence would only make sense to a select few people, she replied, "I know! That was me. I'm Wooster!"

Oh my gosh! Wooster! Live in the flesh. But wait, how?

Reading my expression, Anne Marie enlightened me. "She does have a real name, y'know. This is my friend, Kate. I told her about your blog."

"Ah, now it makes sense. Well, nice to meet you Wooster. Er, Kate," I said.

"You can call me Wooster, sure," she said with a smile.

Anne Marie cranked up the volume on the stereo, the

latest Kylie album playing loud and clear. She then fashioned an improv microphone out of a straw. Her ingenious invention was to bend the crinkly bit of the straw and stick the straw behind her ear so that the bent part hung down near her mouth. It was a huge step up from my hairbrush microphone, plus it could be done on-the-go.

"On a night like this..." she belted out.

I had never seen anything so cool. Mentally filing it under "Impressive Party Tricks," I grabbed a straw for my own microphone.

"I wanna stay forever, stay forever..." Ammo, Wooster, Katrina, and I sang in unison.

This was going to be a great summer.

5

Workin' Hard for the Money

As the summer wore on, I established myself as a regular at a handful of bars. Every night I faithfully drained wine glasses while simultaneously draining my wallet. By day, I explored the famed sites of the city and indulged in various treats from *boulangeries*.

Making the most of my summer was proving to be expensive.

I had sublet my apartment back in St. Louis and scrounged up a bit of savings before leaving. At the time, 5€ was roughly equal to $6.50 so when estimating costs I rounded up. That was fine for small purchases, but going out to bars every night and drinking don't-tell-your-parents-sized quantities was adding up.

And until the checks from my web design projects rolled in, I needed some short term cash. Time to head back to trusty Craigslist!

Amidst many sketchy opportunities, I found a posting

for babysitting a French-Australian couple's kids. I responded to the ad, listing my experience—I'd been babysitting since I was eleven years old[3] and had also worked in a church nursery—and several references. When the reply pinged in my inbox, I could almost taste the wine I could now afford to enjoy. After work of course.

The family lived in the same *arrondissement* as me, close enough to walk. As I made my way to the address the mother had given me, the buildings became noticeably fancier and the streets just a tad cleaner. We may have lived in the same neighborhood, but, wow, we were still worlds apart.

When I reached their classical Parisian building, I buzzed the intercom in the vast marble foyer. A barely-audible click indicated the heavy door was now free to be pushed open. A curved staircase covered in barely-worn red carpeting greeted me. I mounted the stairs to the first floor (using the French method of counting floors, of course), where I thankfully had only one apartment to choose from.

I knocked and heard the rush of little feet towards the door. It opened to one of the cutest kids I've ever seen, who greeted me with a shout of "Veekee!" He'd already learned my name, albeit with an accent.

The mom, Charlotte, was French and the dad, Sam, was Australian. They had met in the US but recently settled in Paris. Their oldest son, Max, the angel-faced door-opener, was a talkative, bilingual four-year-old. Charlotte was holding their other son, Louie, who was 5 months old. *She had a baby five months ago?* My size 6 jeans would drown

---

[3] At that age, I felt totally capable of taking care of another kid. In my first babysitting gig, I cared for a 2-year-old and had to feed her, bathe her, play with her, and put her to bed. Nowadays when I see 11-year-olds they look so darn *young* to me! I can hardly imagine them feeding and bathing themselves, let alone being responsible for someone else. And, yes, I realize I sound like my mom.

her.

Their apartment was expansive but bare. "We're going to Ikea today to furnish the house. We might be a while, so I hope you're free all day?" Charlotte asked. Her English was perfect.

"That is, if we make it out of there alive," Sam added. At that point, I'd never been to Ikea so I laughed along as if I understood. Now, having spent many soul-sucking days at the giant home furnishing chain, I realize he hadn't been joking.

"We have a few more things to do before we're ready to go. You can play with the kids and we'll come say goodbye before we leave," the mom explained as she handed Louie over to me.

"Let me show you our room!" Max shouted, dragging me down the hall.

The apartment was even larger than I thought possible. Three bedrooms, three bathrooms, with a long, bright hallway connecting them. Not to mention the huge living room and dining room I'd already seen. My apartment would fit inside there at least six times.

We played for a bit, giving the kids a chance to get to know me before their parents left. Max selected one of his books and asked me to read it to him. Sure, no problem. Oh, except it was in French. No worries, I can handle a children's book.

"Un jour, un petit chat..." I began.

"No, no!" interrupted Max. "Read it in English!"

Easy for him to say. That would require translating to English as I go, all the while moving at a pace fast enough to hold the attention of a four-year-old. Don't translators charge by the word for this? I trudged on.

"One day, a little cat..." I began again, this time in his preferred language.

"Daddy says it's a kitten," he politely corrected.

Before I could say, "Well, Daddy's not here," his dad

walked in. Not that I would pick a fight with a child. At least not one I'd just met.

"Having fun?" Sam asked. "He keeps you on your toes, huh?"

"You got that right. I'm afraid to hear his French. I'm sure it's better than mine."

"It's definitely better than mine. It's quite embarrassing but I'm happy for his sake. Anyway, you don't need to worry about it. We'd love for you speak English with him. We want him to keep it up now that we've moved from the US."

No problem there. He wasn't in any danger of me choosing to speak French over English any time soon.

Charlotte poked her head around the doorframe. "We're as ready as we'll ever be," she sighed, resigned to her fate of a day at Ikea. "There's a park down the street. Maybe you can take the kids there?" she suggested.

We headed outside together, and the parents kissed the kids goodbye.

"Good luck," I wished them.

"Be good," Charlotte said back, and I wasn't entirely sure if she was talking to the kids, me, or both.

९००

We took a leisurely stroll to the park, enjoying the scenery as Max chattered away. Once through the gates, he dashed off to play while I parked the stroller next to a bench and freed Louie. A cool breeze blew as I leaned back on the bench, Louie on my lap. *Man, it doesn't get much better than this.* Getting paid to play with adorable kids in a beautiful Parisian park? Why thank you, I will!

I wasn't the only one who thought Max was a cutie pie. Before I realized it, five little French girls had gathered around me, asking questions about the handsome new arrival at their playground.

"Comment il s'appelle?" What is his name?

"Il habite où?" Where does he live?

"Il a quel âge?" How old is he?

Next they're gonna ask if he likes long walks on the beach. Not that I'd understand a sentence that complex. I tried to keep up but their French was much better than mine. How's that for bringing you down a notch?

A sweet blonde girl with glasses leaned against my shoulder and sighed dreamily, "Il est très beau." She found him very handsome.

The girls giggled. They were in love.

Max came over to take a break and the girls swooned. He smiled at each one of them as he climbed up next to me on the bench. I handed him a juice box. "You mind sticking around a while to translate for me?"

"I'd love to," he replied.

❧

Since things had gone so well our first day, Charlotte called me back for another babysitting gig. This time, we walked to the Champs de Mars, the large, grassy lawn in front of the Eiffel Tower. Can you imagine growing up down the street from that? The three of us gazed up as we passed. No matter how many times you see it, it's still amazing.

After killing a couple of hours in the nearby playground, we were ready to head home. The boys had already eaten but I was starving. I spotted a *boulangerie* on the way back and popped in to order a sandwich.

"Je prends un sandwich jambon-fromage, s'il vous plaît," I said to the rotund lady behind the counter. As she wrapped it up and I got out my wallet to pay, I noticed the confused look on Max's face.

"You don't speak French," he stated.

"I just did," I couldn't help but reply.

He was quiet for a minute while his brain processed this new information. In his world, his mom spoke French to him and his dad spoke English. When they had lived in the US, people spoke English to him and now that they lived in France, people spoke French. Since I was American and had thus far only spoken English to him, he had slotted me into the "English-speaker" box and it blew his mind that I could speak French, too. Listen a little longer, kiddo, and your mind will be unblown—I'm not that good!

❧

While I did love my nights out at bars, caring for these kids was one of the highlights of my summer. Knowing I had to babysit the next day kept me from partying too hard at night (though the scale is relative—it was still about 10 times harder than my One-Margarita Mom would do). Plus it provided a glimpse into the lives of a real French family.

The kids loved me too. Well, Louie was a bit young to have an opinion so I easily won him over by blowing raspberries on his tummy. But Max liked me because I actually played with him. Many of the other caregivers (whether they were parents or nannies, I don't know) sat on benches, absorbed in a book or a conversation with a friend. But I would often park Louie next to the edge of the playground while he slept and chase Max around until I wore him out.

Then we'd relax over a snack, usually a croissant or *chausson aux pommes*, and talk about the day. To ensure he kept up with his English, his parents wanted me to talk to him a lot. As anyone who knows me will tell you, this was not a problem. And as my mom will tell you, "Vicki started talking at 7 months... and hasn't stopped since." She's a funny one, my mom.

One bright afternoon, Max asked me a question. "What

size t-shirt do you wear?"

"Well it depends on the shirt but I guess I'd say medium." What a funny question. "Why?"

"Because I want to buy you a t-shirt."

Flattered, but knowing I couldn't let him do such a thing, I replied, "Thanks! That's really nice. But I'd rather you keep your money for yourself. That would make me even happier."

"Oh, don't worry, I will. I just wanted you to know how much I like you."

Ha! The kid was good. A French charmer in the making.

6

Sarah's Coming To Town

"I booked my flight!" my step-sister Sarah announced over the crackling long-distance line.

"Awesome! I can't wait to show you around."

Though I had only been living in the city a short while, I was getting used to my new life, picking up baguettes and passing centuries-old architecture. I don't think I'll ever tire of them—Paris is way too awesome for that—but you do reach a point where you go about your daily business without really noticing them. This became most evident on Sarah's visit.

఩఩

Since my parents were divorced, Stephen and I spent our summers with our dad and step-family in sunny Florida. The five-bedroom house was bursting at the seams with our modern-day Brady Bunch of three boys and three girls. We got into all sorts of trouble in very short amounts of time.

Whenever one of the five other kids wanted something (ice cream, movie rentals, a new bike), they would send me to ask Dad because they said I was his favorite. Maybe I was, or maybe they just wanted me to do their dirty work for them. But in the end, it nearly always worked.

One summer when I was about 12, Sarah, 6 months my junior, decided we needed a pool. It took a little more asking than a trip to the ice cream parlor. "Pleeeeeeeeease, Dad? We promise to never ask for anything else ever again and to obey all your rules."

"Here's a rule: just play in the sprinklers. It's the same thing."

Was he kidding? I was going to have to approach this from a different angle. As a thermodynamics engineer, my dad would respond best to straightforward logic. "Dad, look. If you get a pool, we'll swim in it every day and we won't need any other entertainment. But if you don't get us a pool then we'll need to rent movies and go to the arcade and buy lots of other new stuff to be happy. If you think about it, we're actually saving you money."

"I'm not sure your math works out on that, honey."

I looked back at the gang and shrugged my shoulders. Sarah made a motion with her hand, laying it flat and lifting it up high. Huh? Oh... I get it. "We'd settle for an above-ground pool. It's much cheaper."

"Above-ground pool? That's a bit redneck but you're right it's a lot cheaper. I'll think about it." That was as good as a yes in my previous experience.

After the pool was installed and filled (which takes way longer than a kid has patience for), we hopped in and didn't get out all weekend except for bathroom breaks and sunscreen re-applications. At least, I hope everyone got out for bathroom breaks.

On Monday morning, when our parents left for work,

they gave us stern instructions.

"Be careful around the pool and wear sunscreen," my step-mom, Marsha, said.

"And no jumping off the roof into the pool," Dad added.

"Jumping off the roof into the pool? We hadn't thought of that, but now that you mention it, what a great idea!" we collectively thought.

We nodded, our most angelic smiles convincingly plastered to our faces. Not five minutes after our parents were out the door, we were in our swimsuits in the backyard, eyeing the roof.

"I guess a ladder is the best way up," Sarah offered. My older step-brother, Isaac, nodded his agreement.

Propping a ladder against the side of the house would be conspicuous, but then again, so was running off the roof into the pool.

"Are you sure the pool is deep enough?" I asked.

"Yeah, yeah," Sarah assured me.

It didn't seem deep enough to me, but maybe an above-ground pool didn't need to be as deep? We all seemed to be thinking the same thing as we paused in thought. Then Sarah snapped us out of it. "There's only one way to find out!"

One by one, we climbed the ladder. From that angle, the pool sure did seem far away. But once we were up there, no one wanted to chicken out.

"We need a running start in order to clear the edge of the pool," Sarah proclaimed.

I was getting woozier by the minute. I'm not afraid of heights, but I am afraid of knocking my teeth out. Ever since I fell off a row of bleachers and knocked out my front teeth two years earlier (don't worry, they've since been replaced), I'd been afraid of heights-as-tall-as-bleachers. Which was coincidentally the same height as jumping from the roof of a one-story house into a pool.

Without giving it much more thought, Sarah ran off the roof and splashed into the pool. When she surfaced without incident, it gave Isaac, Stephen, and my younger step-brother, Jake, all the encouragement they needed to plunge in after her.

Rebecca, my older step-sister, was not one to be left out and jumped in next.

I was now alone on the roof, my bare feet gripping the gritty roof tiles, my pale, freckly skin exposed for all the neighborhood to see. I had to do it. I couldn't turn back now unless I wanted to be teased the rest of the summer. And I had to do it quickly before I got busted.

Well, you can always get new teeth. I should know.

So I jumped. As I came back up through the water, I was astounded I hadn't broken anything, but I ran my finger across my teeth to be sure. Yep, all there.

Everyone took turns jumping off the roof the rest of the day. Since I'd done it once, I avoided their ridicule and instead passed the day splashing around and dreaming of suntanned skin.

Over dinner that night, Dad asked if we'd behaved. Why do parents ask questions like that? We're never going to answer no.

"You all had fun in the pool today?" It sounded simple enough, but his tone implied it was a test. Everyone looked at me to respond.

"Yep! Thanks for getting it for us."

"No one jumped off the roof?"

"Ha, heh, um, no!" I stammered. How much did he know?

"Then do you have any idea how all that gravel got in there? The gravel that's the exact color of the roof tiles?"

I couldn't hold my innocent expression much longer. "Um, maybe because of the sand? We are in Florida after all," I tried.

"That's not what the neighbor said."

My stomach dropped. He knew! My face was surely red. Everyone else stared down at their plates. How would I get us out of this?

"Which neighbor? The crazy redneck next door?" I'd throw that guy under the bus if it would save us.

"No, Ron across the street." He was triumphant. He knew he had us. "You guys had one rule and you broke it. I bet you were out on the roof ten minutes after we left." *More like five minutes*, we simultaneously thought. We knew not to look at one another or else we'd burst out laughing.

"Now, I can't take the pool away but you're all grounded for two weeks. And no more jumping off the roof. If you do, I'll drain that pool faster than you can swim out of it!"

∞∞

The minute Sarah got off the plane in Paris, we hit the ground running and made the tour of my usual bar circuit. Jetlagged and tipsy, she rattled off all the places she couldn't wait to visit the next day. While I'd seen most of the sites myself, I didn't mind showing her around because you can't ever get too much of Paris.

Halfway through our pub crawl, we passed Notre Dame. I was hurrying because we were late for meeting Lisa and Katrina for karaoke, and Sarah was lagging behind.

"It's just a bit further up this way, Sarah. C'mon!" If we didn't hurry, the karaoke line would be super long and we'd have to sit through a bunch of crappy songs before belting out our own crappy renditions.

"Chill! Can't a girl enjoy the view in peace?" She paused and let out an audible gasp. "Oh my God. Is that Notre DAME? You walk past Notre Dame on your way to the bars? How cool!"

I stopped. I hadn't thought about it but she was right.

That *was* really cool.

"I'm tipsy in front of Notre Dame. Isn't that, like, sacrilegious? But, like, wouldn't it be worse if I walked past without stopping?"

Good point. I suppose karaoke could wait while we had a look-see at the cathedral.

We crossed the pedestrian bridge to get a closer view. It truly is a magnificent church. So ancient, so detailed, so beautiful. No matter how many images you've seen in books or movies, nothing prepares you for how amazing it is up close.

"Buuuuurp." Ahem. Perhaps I shouldn't have finished my last drink so quickly. I silently apologized to God for being so rude before shuffling Sarah along. "We'll come back tomorrow. It will be much better and much less blasphemous. We'll wake up bright and early and conquer the city."

❧

The next day, we woke up groggy and late, but still covered quite a bit of town. We caught up on gossip and reminisced about old times while winding our way through medieval cobblestone streets.

I felt proud to be showing "my city" to a guest and happy to be sharing it with my step-sister. Nothing makes you feel like a local faster. Maybe two weeks ago I was a clueless American making rookie mistakes, but now my step-sister was the rookie and I was the one who knew what was going on.

From the way I'd walk off the Métro before it came to a complete stop (livin' on the edge, baby!) to knowing the owner of the restaurants we dined at, big city living was already second nature.

One of my favorite places, aside from my slew of regular bars, was Refuge des Fondus. Popular with tourists, this rowdy fondue restaurant is usually half-occupied by locals as well. It's hard to say what I like most about the restaurant—from the graffitied walls to climbing over the communal table to sit on the side against the wall—its grungy ambience is a sharp contrast to typical Parisian eateries. It's not unusual for the entire restaurant to sing "Happy Birthday" to a fellow patron, making the rounds in several different languages. And on top of that I get a huge pot of melted cheese? Count me in!

I lied when I said I didn't know what I liked most about the place. Their gimmick is that you drink wine out of baby bottles and this is what stole my heart. It's a guaranteed hit with out-of-town guests, who wear out their camera batteries in various poses with the baby bottles.

In my vast experience, I've discovered that the perfect amount to consume is four baby bottles. Three baby bottles equal one full bottle of wine, so four of the little guys is just the right amount to get you singing "Feliz Compleaños" to the group of Spaniards across the restaurant while still being able to find your way home at the end of the night.

Believe it or not, the owners of this establishment actually like me. I guess because for once, being a tipsy singing girl is the norm. When arriving for a reservation, we always greet each other with *la bise*, the French custom of kissing friends on each cheek. As the long line of hungry patrons outside stares in envy, I can't help but feel cool at being immediately ushered to my table. That might be due more to having a reservation (the restaurant only holds 40 people) than them liking me, but then again they do have my picture posted on the wall. Tough call.

On around my 40th visit, I graffitied my own message on the wall, "La Reine de Fondue." Fondue Queen. Self-proclaimed French royalty. By my 60th visit, I made my own punch card. Surprisingly, they honored it—stamping it each time I came and offering me a free *digestif* when I had filled all ten slots. After my 100th visit, I stopped counting how many times I'd been there. I'm sure I could get a rough estimate by reading my cholesterol chart.

ৼৡ

When Sarah, Lisa, Katrina, and I arrived at the restaurant on the last evening of Sarah's trip, the staff gave us the friendliest of welcomes and immediately brought over the wine. By the time we slammed our 4th baby bottles down on the table, the restaurant had heard the greatest hits from "The Little Mermaid" as well as the crowd-pleasing sing-a-long, "Sweet Caroline." Bellies full of cheese and wine, vocal cords overused and raspy, the evening had been a wild success.

Out of all the places I'd taken her to, the fondue restaurant was the highlight of Sarah's trip. We were crazy kids again, in a different setting. The girl who had once been scared to jump into the pool had now crossed an ocean and was doing just fine.

7

Grab On, It's Going to be a Jerky Ride

The Paris Métro is over 100 years old, the first train barreling down its rails in 1900. By contrast, the city I grew up in was founded in 1988. Heck, even *I'm* older than the city I grew up in.[4]

It amazes me that something so awesomely efficient can be so ancient. Numerous American strip malls have been built and torn down while the Métro keeps transporting millions of passengers day after day.

I love being one of these passengers.

How cool is it to whiz around the city so cheaply? To never have to drive or park. To be able to sit and read while someone else (or, if you're on line 1 or 14, an automated train) takes you to your destination.

---

[4] How is it possible to be older than the city I grew up in, you ask? It's because I was born in Colorado and moved to Missouri later. I love Colorado but consider myself to be "from" Missouri.

Three books about the Paris Métro decorate my bookshelf. While some might consider that three books too many, I'm endlessly fascinated by the topic. There are secret stations, unusual histories behind the station names, and maps galore to bury your head in. The metropolitan network carries 4.5 million people per day and is the second largest subway system in Europe, after Moscow.

Most people appreciate its efficiency and awesomeness as much as I do. But of course there are the jerks. And Métro jerks are a special breed. They know how to get under everyone's skin and ruin the ride.

In increasing order of jerkitude, here are some of my faves:

Reading other people's books.

Settling in for a long ride, these people want to be entertained. Staring off into space would bore them but burdening themselves with their own reading material is out of the question for Monsieur or Madame High-And-Mighty.

So instead they snuggle up next to you and lean over your shoulder to read what you're reading. The joke is on them when they do it to me since I usually read in English. Even if they understand English (plenty of French people do), they can't read as fast as me. I get a special satisfaction out of hearing their disappointed "Oh" when I flip the page before they're done.

Listening to music loudly with headphones.

At the risk of sounding like the old lady I'm rapidly becoming, I want to scream, "You're gonna burst your eardrums!" But they wouldn't hear me over the carefully selected playlist they're gracing the world with. They're never listening to ABBA or George Michael, so I'm never going to want to hear it. So let's turn the volume down a few notches and keep it to ourselves, mmmkay?

Listening to music loudly without headphones.

These people are just douchebags. Makes you wish you never complained about the people *with* headphones.

Too good to touch the pole.

If you're not lucky enough to snag one of the few available seats, then you have to stand. And to avoid being sloshed around the carriage at the slightest bump in the ride, it's a good idea to hold on. Grabbing on to the stranger next to you doesn't work (though that doesn't stop people from trying), so that leaves the shiny-with-other-people's-grime metal poles installed throughout the train cars.

I'm no fan of cooties (then again, who is?) but I don't have a problem holding the pole. When I get off the Métro, I'll simply wash my hands and move on with my life. I don't see the big deal. It's good hygiene to wash your hands several times throughout the day anyway, so this really doesn't put me out.

But there's always a prissypants who has to make a scene about not wanting to touch the pole. Guys can be guilty of this but it's usually a snobby twenty-something girl on her way to someplace more important than you'll ever know.

She'll start out in denial, thinking she won't need to touch the offensive object. As a superior human being, she can manage the toughest twists and turns *en route* without holding on. She shoots you a look that says, "Weakling, your need to grab the germy pole disgusts me." If she's so superior, where's her chauffeur-driven limo?

Then 4.2 seconds later, a jolt from the subway throws her completely off balance and she flails into you. She is still superior, remember, so this is your fault and she will shoot you another look of disdain, this time for having been witness to her embarrassment.

She will release an exaggerated sigh, indicating that

she'll touch the pole but it is way beneath her to do such a thing.

In a futile act of defiance, she'll grab the pole with her thumb and forefinger, as if this somehow means she's not actually touching it. But since two fingers don't sufficiently support the weight of an entire person as the Métro zips around town, she ends up poking you with her other fingers and she slides around the carriage on a banana peel.

I'm not asking her to marry the pole. I'm just asking her to commit to putting one full hand—not 2/5ths of her hand—on it to steady herself so she can stop stabbing me with her raptor nails. She's still gonna have to wash her hands when she gets off, so I don't see the advantage of only clinging on with two fingers.

Eventually she realizes what all of us realized eight stations ago—just grab on to the damn thing with all five fingers and forget about it. By now, I (and the guy next to me) have already read three chapters in my book.

Clipping their fingernails.

It's good these jerkwads plan in advance to bring their nail clippers on the Métro because my retinas were a little too cozy in their eye sockets. Groom away! My eyeballs will catch your stray clippings.

Wearing big coats and ripping your eyelids out.

Innocently ignorant they may be, it doesn't make the situation any less annoying. The offender is usually a tall guy with either a large hood on his anorak or a huge backpack—which he's forgotten extends far past his shoulders. These objects should have a red flag hanging from them and a beeping noise to indicate when the owner is backing up because one quick move to the right and the edge of his coat has knocked the contact lens from your eye. When he jerks back to the left, you'd better move or your cornea's next.

Sleeping on seats with beer cans and a dog.

While this sounds too specific to have occurred more than once, I've in fact seen it several times. A big, hairy scruffy beast with ghastly breath will be sprawled across three seats, preventing you from sitting there (though of course after spotting his puddle of drool, you wouldn't want to anyway). And then there's the dog, standing guard over his snoozing owner, encouraging you to keep a safe distance by squishing yourself up against the opposite side of the car.

Adding charm to the scene is a not-quite-empty beer can rolling around, spilling its contents as the train rocks back and forth, forcing you to hop from foot to foot to avoid drenching your shoes in beer.

Touching other people.

One time I was sitting next to this weirdo. Actually, a lot of times I was sitting next to weirdoes, but I mean, for this particular anecdote, I was sitting next to a weirdo. She was counting under her breath, which doesn't seem that odd compared to all the other occurrences you witness in a big city, but it's still not normal.

Anyway, I had been sitting next to The Count for a few stations when a girl wearing a fur vest hopped on the train. She stood right in front of my royal friend and I, with her back to us. The Count reached out and touched the girl's vest, expressing her thoughts via a succinct "Hrm." The intonation implied "So *that's* what that feels like."

Now, it's not fair to make fun of the mentally unstable so I'll just leave you with this—how many times do you think you've ridden the Métro and someone's touched your clothes without you knowing?

Touching you.

I have no problem with the occasional bump. We're on crowded public transportation—it's inevitable. I always offer a "Pardonnez-moi" afterwards but I don't mind if other people don't. You don't have to apologize for something you might not have even realized you were doing.[5]

I'm talking about people copping a feel. A Métro ticket is less expensive than the local peep-show so these depraved souls are out for a few cheap thrills.

One instance in particular is forever etched into a sad corner of my mind.

I had been riding along, one hand on the pole, one hand on my book, all hands minding my own business. After a station or two, Creep Show sidled up and placed his hand directly above my hand. He had plenty of room to put his hand anywhere else, but no, he had to put it right next to my hand so that we were touching. Are you hoping to reach first base, pal? Because spoiler alert: that ain't gonna happen. In fact, I'll wager a bet that no base-rounding ever happened as a result of touching hands on a Métro pole.

Now, with this guy, I'm pretty sure he was doing it on purpose but it's possible his hand was simply sliding down the pole. I see that happen all the time. And I don't understand it. When I grab the pole (gloved hand or bare) my hand stays right there until the neurons firing in my brain decide to move it. I'm not so generally unaware that I let my hand slide down the pole without noticing. I mean, if you allow your hand to slide without realizing it, that's the first step on a slippery slope to drooling in public and peeing your pants.

Let's hold ourselves to higher standards! Let's take the

---

[5] The London Underground, or The Tube as the locals call it, is even more cramped than the Parisian Métro (hence the nickname). It's virtually impossible to avoid stepping on someone's foot at some point during the journey. It's also virtually impossible for the ever-polite Brits to refrain from apologizing. Your entire ride on the Tube is therefore a chorus of "Sorry's" and "Pardon me's."

miniscule effort required to keep our hand in the same place! I mean, it's not that hard unless you're lubing up your hands before getting on the Métro. Are you lubing your hands before getting on the Métro? Never mind, don't answer that.

At this point I was still on the fence. I was 99% sure he was purposely touching my hand (which must be simply thrilling) but I could still give him the benefit of the doubt. That is, until we got to the bustling Charles de Gaulle Étoile station, where hordes of people got off the Métro. He crushed up against me, under the guise of clearing a path for the other passengers. I wasn't enjoying our one-sided hug but I couldn't get mad because he was courteously making room for people to exit.

But here's the clincher. After everyone had departed, he gave one last thrust and then GOT OFF THE METRO.

Busted!

If he really was just facilitating everyone's disembarkation, his best move would have been to simply go with the flow and leave with everyone else. Staying those few seconds longer proved his guilt, while claiming a little of my innocence.

8

A Hair-Pulling Ride

For every jerk that rides the Métro, there are thankfully ten normal people. If you can tear your eyes away from the bums picking bellybutton lint and the drunks spitting snotwads, you'll witness plenty of heartwarming displays of humanity.

Passengers giving up seats for pregnant women, elderly folks, or less-abled people. A hurried commuter slowing to assist a blind person, a local giving directions to a lost tourist. Pointing out a dropped wallet or chasing after someone who left behind their umbrella. Helping an overtired mother carry her stroller up the stairs or an overburdened traveler push their luggage through the turnstile.

These random acts of kindness show that even amidst the hustle and bustle, these big city inhabitants are more welcoming than their reputation (and my previous chapter, ahem) gives them credit for.

I experienced this warmth one day on my way home from a bit of sightseeing. As I descended the stairs to the platform at the Odéon station, a train was already at the quai, its open doors beckoning me. If I hurried, I could make it before they closed. Except that I don't like to run down stairs (stairs are cousins to bleachers and we know how much I like bleachers). Plus even if I made it *to* the doors in time, it didn't guarantee I'd make it *through* the doors in time.

I decided to take the steps at a leisurely pace and wait on the platform for the next train.

Only problem, this stubborn train wouldn't leave the station! The open doors taunted me. "You can do it," they said. "Or are you too chicken?"

I felt stupid just standing on the platform, but was paralyzed with the fear that if I made a dash for the train, that would be the moment the doors chose to slam on my head.

Which is more embarrassing—staying on the platform when the doors are still open and everyone's wondering why you won't get in, or getting stuck in the doors?

I solved my dilemma by doing both.

After remaining on the quai long enough to look like an idiot, I figured I might as well hop on the train. I covered the distance at a pace brisk enough to get my long blonde hair swinging, and cleared the doors right as they were closing. Whew, that was close.

All eyes were on me, no doubt wondering what took me so long to take the plunge. I looked for an open seat, anxious to get out of everyone's line of sight. I took a step and was rudely yanked back. "What the...?"

My hair was stuck in the doors! No problem. I'd just pretend I wanted to stand here. I only had to wait until the next station.

But suddenly, the train lurched around a bend, throwing all the passengers to the side with it. The movement pulled my hair enough to sting but not enough to set me free. I winced. A kind-faced elderly man noticed my predicament and placed one arm on each of my shoulders. Normally, this would be way too intimate a pose for two strangers, but I graciously accepted his help. As the train swayed, he held me in place so that I might survive the experience with a few hairs left on my head.

Our faces were close. Should I say something? My French wasn't up to the task but it seemed rude to remain silent. I could at least start with the basics.

"Merci, monsieur," I said.

"De rien," he replied with a smile.

Man, I thought the conversation would flow once I got started. It was only about a minute between stations and we'd already killed some time, so I just smiled until we arrived at the next station.

Mercifully, the train pulled in to Sèvres-Babylone and as the doors opened, my hair fell in one big whoosh down my back. The man removed his arms from my shoulders and tipped his head.

"Encore merci, monsieur. Bonne journée." I wished him a good day as I slunk over to an empty seat in embarrassment. I glanced around the car and saw that everyone had already moved on. Some were reading, some were playing games on their phones. None of them were snickering about the silly girl whose hair got stuck in the doors.

I caught the eye of my elderly knight in shining armor and he winked, a sweet innocent wink that said "See, it's alright."

And it was.

෧෫

The Métro and I were great friends, but occasionally my partying would end at an awkward time between when the last Métro ran (around 1:30 am) and the first one of the next day roared down the tracks (about 5:45 am).

A few times I covered the three mile journey home on foot. Paris is surprisingly safe for such a large city, but walking home alone after a few drinks is still a risk I preferred to avoid.

So occasionally I'd have to take a taxi home. This always promised to be an adventure.

"Bonsoir, monsieur!" I'd say. Ninety-nine times out of a hundred it would be a guy driving (the female taxi drivers usually only work during the day). "Dans le quinzième, s'il vous plaît. 20 rue Blomet."

The winning formula: be polite, indicate the general direction you're heading by mentioning the *arrondissement* first, then give the street name. But no matter how perfectly I thought I got through this part, my accent always gave me away. The booze coursing through my veins probably didn't help either.

Assuming I was just another drunk American tourist (to be fair, they weren't totally off the mark), the taxi drivers would prolong the journey, taking needless detours as the price on the meter skyrocketed. I lived near the Eiffel Tower but the trip home didn't necessitate passing it. Nonetheless, I'd gazed up at the iron structure from the back seat countless times, enjoying its beauty but not the price I was paying for it.

"I got taken for another lap round the Eiffel Tower last night," I lamented to Anne Marie over a glass of wine.

"Ha, ha, that's the worst. I've seen Notre Dame a million times on account of that." She wiped down the bar and restacked a fallen pile of cardboard coasters. "I had to learn me way around. You have the right to tell them which way you wanna go and they have to listen, y'know."

No, I didn't know! "Really? Like, street by street?"

"Well, I can't be arsed to tell them street by street but you can give them the main roads. And definitely tell them not to pass that bloody Eiffel Tower. It's not even lit up that time of night so I dunno what they're playing at."

A customer came in and Ammo walked over to take his order. I contemplated this new information. Surely I could study a map and get the general gist of it, especially since I knew the way on foot. It might be different by car on account of all the one-way streets and construction, but I could memorize a few acceptable routes.

As for mastering how to say it in French, I already knew "right," "left," "straight," and "please" so I was in pretty good shape. Throw in a few street names and I'd be fine.

A few nights later, I tried my plan. I'd been out with Lisa on the other side of town and had a smidge too much to drink. There was no way I'd make it to 5:45, so taxi it was.

As I glanced down the street, I saw a taxi approaching. What luck! I got in and confidently, but politely, told the driver where I was going and my preferred route. We were off!

Almost immediately, I felt sick to my stomach. I've always been a queasy person and I get carsick easily. The two shots of Jaeger that had sounded like such a good idea earlier sloshed violently around my wine-filled belly each time we took a turn.

This was going to be a long ride.

I tried to focus straight ahead while keeping an eye on which roads the taxi driver took. I might not have been sober but I'd be damned if I was going past the Eiffel Tower again!

I still felt woozy. To distract myself, I counted prime numbers up to one hundred[6]. It requires just enough

---

[6] Don't worry, I counted silently in my head. If the taxi driver ever wrote a book about his life in Paris, I wouldn't want to appear in his "Weirdo Passengers" chapter.

concentration to divert your attention without being too difficult. It usually worked. That night, however, I only made it to 47 before realizing I needed to vomit.

How far from home am I? With Esplanade des Invalides on the horizon, I calculated I had a good ten minutes before we'd be in my neighborhood.

Stay calm. Hold it for five more minutes, then you can get out and walk the rest of the way. The fresh air will feel great! And then if you need to, you can puke.

Big mistake. Just thinking the word made me sick. Crap, crap, crap. I looked up again. We were stopped at a red light. *It's now or never!*

I opened the car door, leaned out, did my business, then quickly slammed the door shut. Not too shabby! I didn't mess up the car and I kept my seatbelt on the whole time. And, hey, the light is still red so I didn't even hold up traffic. As I was about to pat myself on the back, I caught the driver's eye in the rear view mirror. He clearly wasn't as impressed with my performance as I was.

"C'est dégeulasse, mademoiselle! Vous êtes bourré!" That's disgusting! You're drunk!

At this moment I realized he was about to head past the Eiffel Tower. Oh *hell* no! I may have puked out of his car but I still know when I'm getting screwed.

"Je suis desolée, monsieur. J'ai mangé quelque chose bizarre. Pouvez-vous prendre à gauche?" He clearly didn't buy my excuse that I'd eaten something weird but by following my directions he'd get me home (and therefore out of his car) much sooner.

I'm not sure which one of us was more relieved when I finally exited the car. I gave him a huge tip (hey, that's one good thing about Americans) and wished him a *bonne soirée.* It had been a good evening, indeed.[7]

---

[7] Well, a good evening for one of us. I still might end up in his book someday.

9

No Worries, Mate

Parisian bakeries are world-famous for being awesome. French women are world-famous for being skinny. The two must have never met because I don't see how these women stay so svelte when there are thousands of calories staring them in the face.

And *boulangeries* are more prolific in Paris than Starbucks are in the United States. On a stroll to the post office (they have an absurd amount of those, too) it's not uncommon to pass three or four bakeries. How on earth can you resist?

With time I've mellowed and am usually able to escape with just one carb-laden item. But in the beginning, I had to peel my face away from the glass as the *boulangère* called, "Client suivant!" Next!

"Une baguette, s'il vous plaît." A baguette was mandatory so that I could make a sandwich or spread some cheese on it or carry it around town to look like a local. To go with it I could order a croissant or a *pain au chocolat* (which is like a croissant but with chocolate running through it) or a *suisse au chocolat* (which is like a *pain au chocolat* with some creamy, wonderful, artery-clogging substance running through it). It was the toughest choice of my day.

The baker interrupted my thoughts. "Avec ceci?"

To my not-yet-fluent ears, it sounded like "Avec soucis?" *"With worries?" I guess it's a weird take on the Australian "No worries" phrase.* Glad that the baker had no worries about my baguette, I ordered a croissant, too. The baker gave me an odd look but that was nothing new—it happened nearly every time I spoke French. I paid and went on my way. Not the smoothest of transactions, but I had warm, buttery, gluten-y products in my hands. All was good.

Later that night, I stopped in at Ammo's bar. Sipping the froth off the top of my beer, I asked, "So what's with the bakers here saying 'avec soucis'? Is it some Australian thing?"

By the blank stare on her face, I knew I had said something stupid. "Avec SOO-see, you're saying? Ha ha ha ha ha ha ha ha!"

That was maybe one "ha" too many. I got it. I must have been wrong about something. But what?

"They're saying 'avec SUH-see', you know, like 'Anything else with that?'"

Oh. Ohhhhh. *Ohhhhhhhhhhhh.* Now it made sense. And now I realized just how dumb I had looked. Not only did I brush off their "Anything else?" question, but I'd replied by ordering *something else.* Why haven't these people kicked me out of their country yet?

The best I could do is learn from it and do better next time. I'd have to get used to embarrassing myself until I mastered the language.

Ready for another drink, I asked Anne Marie for a pint

of lager. "Avec SOO-see?" she replied.

Well played.

10

Royale with Cheese

Being a freelance web designer, I needed an internet connection to work. But my apartment had only intermittent access and since I was subletting, I couldn't call the internet service provider to sort it out.

Not that I would call anyway. If I can't even figure out how to order a baguette at the *boulangerie*, face to face, a technical conversation with a phone operator would be a disaster.

So, like it or not, I became a regular at the local McDonald's, home of hamburgers and free Wi-Fi. I would do as much work as I could at home, then dash out to McDo (as the French affectionately call it) to get my connection. If the restaurant was moderately busy, I could usually hide out and use the Wi-Fi without buying anything. But if it was empty, I had to make a purchase to avoid getting busted, and if it was busy I had to make a purchase to avoid feeling guilty about taking a table from a paying customer.

As a result, I became quite familiar with the French McDonald's menu.

While there is nearly an infinite selection of better restaurants to choose from in this wonderful city, I have to say that McDonald's still isn't bad. In fact, the quality is way better than in the US. The chicken looks like it might have come from an animal at some point. (Please don't shatter the illusion for me if that's not true. I'd like to still be able to eat there occasionally.) The ice cream is the perfect treat on a warm day. And the coffee, well, you could do worse.

However, I witnessed two uniquely French aspects that I will never understand.

The first was when the ever-popular Royale with Cheese[8] was covered by a sign stating "Victime de son succès." Victim of its own success. Essentially, the item was so popular that they had run out. Props for the creative phrasing.

But once I thought about it, which I had plenty of time to do since people never decide what to order until they're at the register, I recognized a few problems with this.

First, how do you run out of one of your most popular items? You know people are going to order it, so you should make sure you have enough in stock. You sell hamburgers. You should always have hamburgers for sale. It's quite simple.

Second, the sign was not some hastily-scrawled note written on a scrap of paper. It was typed and laminated indicating that this was likely not the first time, nor the last time, it would be used. Maybe they should spend more time stocking up on hamburgers and less time laminating

---

[8] For all of you who've seen "Pulp Fiction," you already know this is what the French call a Quarter Pounder since they use the metric system over here and "don't know what the f*ck a quarter pounder is."

signs.

Third, I noticed that the Royale with Cheese & Bacon was still available. Wait... what? If you have a Royale with Cheese & Bacon then by definition you have a Royale with Cheese. It's right there in the name. How can you run out of Royales with Cheese but still make them with bacon? That's like saying you've run out of small fries but still have medium fries.

Which brings me to my second point of confusion, which I'm now realizing is pretty much the same point but let's just go with it.

The menu boasted a huge sign announcing "Le Retour deu Double Cheese." The double cheeseburger is back.

How exciting! That's my favorite.

You may think that one cheeseburger plus one cheeseburger equals the same amount of pleasure as a double cheeseburger but some crazy math occurs with double cheeseburgers and they end up being more than twice as good as one cheeseburger. It has something to do with all that uninterrupted cheese and meat stuffed together between just one bun.

Ahem. Where was I?

Right. "Le Retour de Double Cheese." As exciting as it was, it seemed like we had a "Royale with Cheese & Bacon" situation on our hands. If they have more than one cheeseburger in their establishment (and I hope they do or else they'll have disgruntled stockholders on their hands) then they have enough for a double cheeseburger.

So I don't understand why they're heralding the return of the double cheeseburger when it's *always been there*. Is it some twisted mind game they're playing? They pretend they've taken it away to make us crave it that much more?

Behind the heavy mahogany doors of the McDonald's boardroom:

Chairman #1: We need to increase profits. What new products can we offer? Salads?

Chairman #2: You make me laugh. No, the question is not what new products we can offer, but which products we can take away. For starters, let's take the beloved double cheeseburger off the menu and build a huge demand for it. Our heartbroken customers will try to fill the void by buying two cheeseburgers, but they won't be satiated. Soon, we'll wake to the chants of "Double! Double! Double!" As the chants grow louder, the mutinous maniacs will work themselves into a frenzy, banging on the store windows. The day the double cheeseburger returns, they'll be so grateful they will become customers for life.

Chairman #1: Er, wouldn't it be more profitable to always offer the more expensive product?

Chairman #2: Where's the fun in that?

Whatever their reasoning, at least I can now sleep at night knowing my favorite product is back.

By the way, if I ever form an indie rock band, remind me to name it Mutinous Maniacs.

ço∙ಲ

When not taking advantage of free Wi-Fi and overanalyzing French signage practices, I enjoyed dining in "real" restaurants. At the end of my street sat a rustic restaurant specializing in southwestern French cuisine. The menu boasted generous servings of comfort food, my favorite of which was a humongous salad served out of what resembled a dog's bowl.

That makes it sound unappetizing but it was downright delicious. It was everything a salad should be—that is, a few pieces of lettuce weighted down with sautéed potatoes, country-cured ham, and hearty chunks of Roquefort and Cantal cheese. Served with a lightly-chilled glass of red wine to wash it down.

My friend Lydia joined me one evening to see what the fuss was about. Her dark bouncy curls and cheerful smile were the same as they'd been back in junior high, where we'd both known of each other but weren't actually friends.

In fact, we didn't officially meet until a mutual friend came to Paris to visit and introduced us. After the requisite trip to Refuge des Fondus, we were bonded for life. Our mutual friend returned home but Lydia and I stayed in touch. I enjoyed having someone from back home who instantly understood the differences between life in St. Louis and Paris. And shared my love of cheese.

"How cozy!" Lydia exclaimed as the waiter showed us to our table. "Oh my goodness, is that a *salad?*" Several diners were already digging into their scrumptious feast, huge grins spread across their faces. "I'm definitely ordering that."

"You would like zee Eenglish menu, zen? You are Americans, *non?*" the waiter asked.

"Oui, nous sommes Américaines." I answered. Great. I knew where this was going.

"And you are visiting Paris? Where are you from?" he continued in a heavy accent.

Lydia and I both said "St. Louis" at the same time.

"Ah, oui, St. Louis. I know this place. *Louisiane*, non? Super. I will get zee menu en anglais."

Damn. The English menu always had translations that were just enough off that you didn't know what they were saying. Some stuff simply can't be translated. Like, *foie gras* is still *foie gras* in English. No one wants to order "fatty goose liver" but *foie gras* sounds more worthy of the exorbitant price.

And where certain phrases sound wonderful in French, they lose a lot when Anglicized. I've seen "langue de bœuf sauce piquante" translated as "language of cow hot sauce." Not that "beef tongue with spicy sauce" sounds much more appetizing but at least it's recognizable.

The best, which I've seen several times, is "salade

d'avocat," or "salad of lawyers." It's not their fault the French language uses the same word for "avocado" and "lawyer," but it seems like the type of thing you'd want to check before printing and laminating your menus.

We ordered off the English menu anyway, and passed the evening in a blur of indulgent food and copious amounts of wine. I recall a tasty after-dinner drink (or three) comprised of white wine, wild berry liqueur and cognac. I'm sure I no longer had any control over the volume of my voice.

At one point, I became aware that I'd been sitting with my elbow propped up on my neighbor's chair. Parisian restaurants wedge their patrons in cramped spaces, but they don't expect you'll get *that* close. Whoops.

Time to call it a night. I shakily stood up, knocking my chair over in the process. And since my oversized handbag had been hanging over the back of the chair, it plunged to the tile floor with a loud thud. Double whoops.

I was paralyzed with embarrassment, unable to bolt out of there as I so desperately wanted to do. I mentally reviewed the contents of my purse, determining if I needed anything or if I could make a run for it now and come back the next day to retrieve it.

Lydia interrupted my thoughts. "I know what you're thinking. But no. Pick up your purse and let's go."

Red-faced from the wine and embarrassment, I snatched up my bag, set the chair straight, and apologized to everyone at the neighboring tables. I left a flurry of cash on the table, enough to more than cover the meal plus tip.

In hindsight, I probably shouldn't have had so many after-dinner drinks. Then again, they shouldn't make them taste like Kool-Aid if they don't want me to order fifty of them.

Who can win a fight against wild berry liqueur?

֍

Living in a big city, there are lots of take-away options as well, which is perfect for the nights when you want to relax on the *canapé* instead of sitting through a three-hour restaurant meal.

One such evening I was in the mood for Japanese. I recalled a sushi place that had opened nearby and decided to check it out. After browsing their overpriced menu, I settled on a salmon roll and an ahi tuna roll. I paid nearly two hours' worth of babysitting for them and then waited an absurdly long time for something that didn't need to be cooked.

"Veekee!" they called as my order came up. "Voulez-vous des baguettes avec ceci?"

Huh? I'd learned the "avec ceci" part after my bakery adventures, but baguettes? What on earth would I want a baguette for? I'm eating sushi! Maybe it's compensation for their prices. Like, they know you'll still be hungry so they pair it with bread in a lame attempt to make up for it? Odd. Plus with all the wonderful *boulangeries* in Paris, I'm not sure a Japanese take-away is the place to get a baguette.

"Non, merci," I replied, picking up the sack.

"Vous êtes sûre? Pas de baguettes?" he insisted.

Was I missing something? Why was this guy trying to ram a baguette down my throat? Maybe I should have said yes and taken the darn thing but since I'd already rejected him once, I stuck to my guns.

"Non, merci. Bonne soirée."

When I returned home, I laid out my priccy delicacies. I emptied the contents of a soy sauce packet into a makeshift tray, and was about to swirl wasabi into it when I realized they had forgotten my chopsticks. After spending all that money for a miniscule portion of fish and rice they could have at least provided the utensils required to eat it.

I rummaged around my kitchen drawers until I found a pair of reusable chopsticks. Lucky I had those!

The meal was tasty but my stomach growled as I

grasped the last piece of sushi with my chopsticks. Maybe I should have taken the baguette after all.

ဪ

A few days later, Lydia and I stopped in at Anne Marie's bar. It's a good thing I stumbled onto that place or I don't know how I'd spend all my time. Or all my money.

"How you gettin' on?" she asked.

"Fine, for the most part. I'm finding my way around and making the most of my time here." I filled her in on the chopsticks incident. "It's not a huge deal, but still. If I'm spending the GNP of a small nation on take-away Japanese, I'd at least like some utensils with it."

She gave me a look I was quickly recognizing as the you-idiot-you've-done-it-again look. Uh-oh. What have I done now?

"Maybe you should have asked them for chopsticks," she offered.

"Yeah, I suppose so. I just assumed they were in the bag."

"And if you were to ask for chopsticks, how would you have asked?"

I'm always embarrassed to speak French to another English speaker. With French people, I have no choice. But with English-speakers I'd rather not look stupid if I can avoid it.

Though I sensed it was a bit late for that.

"Um, maybe 'Avez-vous des …'" I paused and thought for a second. "Hrm, I guess I don't know the French word for 'chopsticks'."

"It's 'baguettes'."

You have got to be kidding me. No wonder the cashier had insisted so strongly on the baguettes. Here I thought he was trying to Frenchify my Japanese meal while he'd been thinking I planned to eat with my cavewoman hands.

"Can you come with me everywhere I go?" I asked, only half-joking. "I can't seem to get anything right."

"Nah, nah, you're doing fine. I'm just takin' the piss," she assured me. At least I think it was meant to assure me, but I couldn't bring myself to tell her I didn't understand her expression, even though it was in English!

Anne Marie left us to wash some glasses, while I stared into my glass and drifted off in thought. I wonder what my family is doing right now back home. They're certainly speaking English with normal phrases that everyone understands. No one's 'taking the piss' or imposing baguettes on other people. Life is so easy for them.

As a perfectionist, it was hard for me to be so wrong all the time. How easy it would be to go back home! No language barrier, no foreign city, no daily obstacles over the simplest tasks.

Then again, it wouldn't be Paris. What would I do without the fresh baguettes I'd grown accustomed to (the bread, of course—not chopsticks)?

And even if it was hard, I had to admit it was satisfying when I said something correctly in French and was met with a comprehending nod instead of a "Huh?" And anyway, what's life without a few challenges? *I guess it's OK to not get everything right all the time, because I'm having the time of my life.*

Confessions as Summer Ends

After clicking "send" on an email to my mom, I crossed my fingers until the weak internet shot my message into cyberspace, then shut down my computer. I was done working for the day and needed to unwind before heading out for the evening. Quality journal time.

I walked home barefoot from a bar, having lost both flip flops in two separate incidents. Dirty from the dance floor, my feet were in embarrassing shape. Yet I miraculously arrived home with feet cleaner than I'd ever seen. The fresh rain combined with the abrasive sidewalks gave me a free French pedicure.

Sometimes, just sometimes, I might drink a

wee bit too much. But when you're broke and on a budget and someone offers you free shots, what are you supposed to do?

I was supposed to stay for three months. But I think I always knew I would stay a little longer, despite the crazy Frenchies. Or maybe because of them.

11

Could This Be It?

Strolling down the gorgeous Boulevard Saint Germain, you're surrounded by posh buildings, all about six or seven stories high. Built in the typical Parisian style of the mid 19th century when Haussmann revamped most of Paris, the buildings are similar in a good way. Their homogenous façades unify the city and ensure that no matter how many dogs or drunks urinate in the street, the overall scene is still beautiful.

I'm even more fascinated by the buildings' interiors. If you're lucky, you can catch a glimpse inside an apartment on a lower level, or at nighttime if someone's light is on you can sneak a peek at their ornate ceilings and elaborate light fixtures.

In passing these apartments I imagine the rest of their house. Does it have original hardwood floors? Decorative crown molding? People walking around in their undies? (The answer to all three is usually "yes.")

I try to guess which sites of the city they can see from their balcony. The Eiffel Tower lit up at night? The beautiful dome of the Sacré Cœur Basilica? The funky (putting it nicely) exterior of the Pompidou Center? There are some truly amazing places to live in Paris, and if I ever win the lottery[9] my first order of business is to scoop up one of these gems.

Until then, I'll have to make do with middle class apartments. While I'll never be able to afford a five-bedroom number overlooking the Luxembourg Gardens, I do still recognize that even the crappiest Parisian apartment is still a Parisian apartment and therefore will always have a certain charm.

The apartment I sublet during my first summer was one of the nicest I've had in Paris. It offered a great balance of old and new, function and beauty. At the time I thought it was small and expensive, but with years of apartments behind me now, I realize I had it pretty good. Twenty square meters for 500€ a month was a steal.

After that summer, I sort of fell into a relationship with a French-Brazilian guy, Pierre. He was tall, dark, and handsome (it's a cliché for a reason), not to mention exotic. We hit it off instantly, despite not having much in common.

He also had a relatively large apartment by Parisian standards. Since I was in need of a new place after my sublet was up, he offered to let me move in with him. His family owned the 38-square-meter apartment but as they lived in Brazil, they let him live in it rent-free. My contribution was to cover the condo fee, which was way lower than what I'd have to pay in rent somewhere else. What a deal!

---

[9] Of course, you have to play to win. And as a math nerd I know the probability of me winning is less than being struck by lightning. Then again, I've been struck by lightning so maybe that improves my odds?

But that's the thing. While we stayed together for three years, a part of me wonders if it had to do with the deal. Would we have moved in together so quickly if apartments weren't so difficult to get? Would we have stayed together so long if the situation wasn't so darn affordable? It's not like we ever actively sat down and weighed the financial pros and cons of our relationship, but on some level it must have always been there.

As I stroll past these ornate apartment buildings and catch a glimpse inside I wonder, *Are these people as happy as they appear from the outside?*

When you read ads for apartment rentals and then you see the exorbitant price next to them, it's easier to understand why people stay together longer than they should.

"Pierre's caught up with work," I told Anne Marie as she poured me a pint. I'd gone out by myself yet again while my boyfriend stayed home to work.

"Oh yeah, right, your 'boyfriend'," Ammo snarked.

"What?" I shouted defensively. Just because she'd never met him didn't mean he didn't exist. Since he worked from home, it was hard for him to separate his work time from his personal time. He'd often not look up from his computer until 10 at night.

"Nothing, nothing. Don't get your panties in a twist. I'm just saying I've still never met the guy. I've never seen the Loch Ness Monster either, but I guess it could exist."

Was it really that bad? Now that I thought about it, Lydia had also joked about my "invisible" boyfriend.

"Gimme a shot of vodka, and pour one for yourself, Ammo." I pushed my relationship out of my mind, and somehow didn't get around to thinking about it for several years.

I still consider my time with Pierre time well spent. We shared some fun memories and I learned a lot about what I was looking for. On the more practical side, I was able to extend my stay in Paris without going broke. I had a sense of stability, more permanent than the apartment I had sublet for the summer. Living in Paris was not a prolonged vacation, it had become my life.

§∞§

When our relationship hit the three-year mark, Pierre and I took a trip to Italy. I pragmatically thought that after living together for that long, the next logical step was marriage. I never stopped to think about whether I actually wanted it.

"Have you had a chance to pack? We leave tomorrow." I had just gotten home from the gym and was planning to pack after hopping in the shower.

"Yep. The suitcase is in the bedroom with my stuff," he replied.

The bathroom filled with steam as I daydreamed about Pierre proposing to me in Italy. As I toweled off, the sight of the loose mismatched tiles snapped me back to reality. We were going to have to redo this room once we were married.

As I threw on my pajamas, I noticed the open suitcase laying on the floor. Sure enough, all his stuff was in there. *Including a ring?*

It couldn't hurt to have a peek, could it? I had performed in local theater productions back home, so I was sure I could act surprised when he popped the question. He would never know I'd been digging around the bag.

I peeked my head out the bedroom door and saw him firmly planted in front of his computer, a huge stack of expense receipts to submit. I'd be safe for at least another hour.

I only needed about thirty seconds. Rooting through the suitcase I found enough clothes for three days and one pair of flip flops. Not only was there no ring, there weren't even enough clothes for our week-long trip. *Ah, so maybe he's not done packing yet!*

"Hey, honey? You done packing? I'm wondering how much room I have to work with," I fibbed. I mean, I did need to know but that's not why I was asking.

"Yep, all done," he shouted from the living room.

What? I've seen five-year-olds pack more thoroughly than this, but the last thing a man wants is a glimpse of his future nagging wife so I let it be.

Maybe he's hiding the ring until the last minute because he knows I'll dig through the suitcase. But that didn't explain his choice of clothes. All he packed was casual wear. Hardly dressy enough to go out to dinner! Not that you have to propose in a restaurant. *Oh! That's totally it. He's avoiding clichés. I bet he's got a huge surprise planned!*

I forced myself to forget about it and decided that for once in my life I would relax and see what happened.

Well, I was so busy relaxing that all of a sudden it was the end of the trip before I realized he hadn't proposed. On the flight back to Paris, I reflected on the situation. Part of me was mad that he had let this great opportunity slip by. But another part of me wondered, *Is this even what I want?*

It took a few more months for us to realize the inevitable. I had a two-week business trip to the US, then planned to meet Pierre in Brazil for two weeks of vacation (part business/part fun for him). We agreed that by the end of the month, we needed to determine where we were headed as a couple. During that month we'd have time together and time apart, time with our families and time abroad. It would give us every opportunity to think things through.

After a lovely two weeks in my homeland, I took off for Brazil, no more certain about what I wanted than before I left Paris. Maybe I'd see things differently in the southern hemisphere.

First stop—a village in the state of Minas Gerais, where the sugar cane for Pierre's company was farmed and then refined into the tasty, if strong, cachaça liquor they bottled and distributed worldwide. One of his colleagues, Tiago, gave us an in-depth tour of the sugar cane plantation (complete with guys hacking down the plants with machetes, hi-YA!) and the pristine refinery. The entire operation was self-sufficient, even to the point where the workers ate lunch that had been made from ingredients grown on their property. That's like the total opposite of how we do things back in St. Louis. I was fascinated.

Tiago pointed out various plants on the farm, mostly speaking Portuguese, but throwing in English where he could. I understood most of it, mainly because I knew what a chicken and a mango looked like. But then he pointed out what I'm pretty sure was a "cashew bush." Huh? Big fruity objects, kind of like pears, hung from the thin branches. I didn't see any cashews but maybe I had misunderstood.

Our tour finished in the canteen, just in time for lunch. Platters of chicken and mango greeted us, proving they really did get the ingredients from their farm. Served alongside the meal was an unusual juice that I couldn't quite place. It was murky like grapefruit juice but tasted extremely tart. *Yowza*, I thought, as I couldn't help pulling a face.

Noting my expression, Tiago enlightened me. "It's *caju* juice. You like?"

"Cashew juice? I don't get it. How can you make juice out of a cashew?"

"Remember *caju* bush this morning?" He pointed out the window to the garden we'd visited earlier. "It comes from there."

Ah, so I had heard correctly. "So... it's a fruit? But where's the nut part?"

"Technically, it's not nut. But it comes from same fruit.

It hangs on bottom. We keep fruit for us and export nut. The fruit, it lasts only short time, so it's not good for export."

Amazing. Who knew that a cashew was actually a fruit (and one you could make juice out of, at that!) and that what we called cashews were actually cashew nuts? Except technically they weren't even nuts at all. Man, there was a whole world of stuff I didn't know!

❧❧

Our next stop was the grand city of São Paulo. As a native of Rio de Janeiro, Pierre inherently disliked São Paulo. Kind of like how I detest the Chicago Cubs since I'm a St. Louis Cardinals girl.

Ever the loyal girlfriend, I agreed to dislike São Paulo, too. But once I saw it, I changed my mind. Skyscrapers stretched as far as the eye could see and bartenders crushed fresh limes into caipirinhas at every bar. I could get used to this!

Except that I couldn't.

My Portuguese was virtually non-existent, except for the swear words I had learned from watching football matches. And without Tiago the Tour Guide I needed Pierre by my side at all times to translate. Not to mention the city isn't safe, yet another reason I needed him with me all the time. And unfortunately he was busier with work than he'd anticipated.

Over a quick breakfast before one of Pierre's meetings, I bravely ordered in Portuguese. "Um sanduíche de queijo e suco de abacate, por favor." Mmm, a cheese sandwich and pineapple juice.

Minutes later, the waitress rushed to our table and set down a glass of green gelatinous weirdness. As she dashed off, the substance was still jiggling.

"I think this is for someone else," I hopefully suggested

to Pierre.

"Huh?" he said, looking up from his phone. "No, it's *suco de abacate*, like you asked for." He resumed texting whoever was so important on the other end.

I was pretty sure this ooze wasn't pineapple juice. Then again, I hadn't even known cashew juice existed until a few days ago. Why is juice so complicated?

"Are you *sure* it's pineapple juice?" I wanted to make sure the order was wrong before bothering the waitress.

"Pineapple juice? Who said anything about pineapple juice? You ordered avocado juice."

Gag me! "I would never order avocado juice. Up until two seconds ago I didn't even know such a thing existed."

"You ordered *suco de abacate*," he said, pronouncing the avocado like 'ah-buh-cash'. "Pineapple juice is *suco de abacaxi*." The subtle difference sounded more like "ah-buh-cash-ee."

You've got to be kidding me. The difference between a delicious glass of citrus goodness and this putrefaction in front of me was a simple "ee" sound?

Knowing I was wrong but still mad about it (or perhaps mad *because* I was wrong), I tried to blame it on him. "I like avocados but you *know* I hate them sweetened with sugar. And you *know* I love pineapple juice. So why would I order avocado juice? Isn't it more likely that I simply said it incorrectly? Last time I checked, Portuguese isn't my native language."

"Well, you said *abacate*. Now I'm supposed to be a mind reader?"

This conversation wasn't going to be easy if he kept being right. Luckily, for probably the first and only time in my life, I had the perfect response. "OK, so next time we're at a bar and you order a 'turd' pint of beer instead of a 'third' pint, I hope they bring you a big steaming glass of shit!"

"That's real mature." His chair screeched as he scooted

it back. "I'm outta here." He got up and started to walk away.

"Oh *that's* real mature, just walking away!"

But he kept on going. I was in deeper shit than his third pint. How was I going to manage on my own all day? Why couldn't I have picked the fight *after* our trip? Or at least after breakfast.

As I looked down at the glass of avocado juice, it stared defiantly back at me. "Ha, ha, your Portuguese sucks and there's nothing you can do about it and now you're all alone!" it said. A tear snuck out of the corner of my eye.

When the waitress came by with my sandwich, I ordered a *suco de abacaxi*, as if all along I'd intended on ordering two similarly-named drinks. Paying for a beverage I had no intention of consuming was easier than trying to exchange it, especially when it was my fault for messing up the order in the first place.

I lingered over my sandwich and my freshly-squeezed pineapple juice, postponing the inevitable trip outside. If things had gone this poorly over breakfast, how on earth would I survive the rest of the day? I couldn't blame Pierre for leaving a fight to go to work—he was on a business trip after all—but his actions gave me a sneak peek of our future together. Would I always take a backseat to his job? Was I destined to puppy-dog him around everywhere, begging for scraps of attention?

With a deep breath, I composed myself and headed to the cashier. I handed him my diner's card, which is this cool gadget popular in Brazilian restaurants. They give you one when you walk in and swipe it in a handheld machine when you order, keeping a running total. Super convenient when you need to order several juices.

Outside, the city seemed so much bigger. So did the insects. Worms morphed into snakes and beetles were the size of my clenched fists. I hurried back to the hotel as fast as my untanned legs would carry me.

Cooped up in my hotel room, bright sun taunting me through the window, I came to the conclusion we had to break up. One day Pierre would want to move back to Brazil, and after today's experience I knew I would never want to go with him. Paris was my new home and I didn't want to start over somewhere else. And I didn't want to follow him. Go *together*, maybe. But it just didn't feel like we were together.

ॐॐ

A few days later, safely back in a land where I knew how to order *jus d'ananas* and never *jus d'avocat*, we had "the talk." It was amicable, and luckily he had six weeks of business travel planned, giving me time to find a new place.

I definitely wouldn't miss that ugly bathroom. Or the ugly kitchen. Or the oversized bed in the undersized bedroom. Or... well, OK. I would miss everything a bit. That apartment had been my home for three years. I had built my life in France while living there. I was sad to leave it behind. But it would be lovely to say goodbye to that turquoise bathtub.

12

Should I Stay Or Should I Go Now?

In a stroke of good luck, or maybe karma, my next apartment was a short-term loaner from a friend, Chris, whom I had met through volunteer work. She lived in the suburbs with her husband but kept a pied-à-terre in the city. It sat conveniently around the corner from Pierre's apartment so I loaded up my suitcases, took one last look around my former residence, then wheeled noisily down the block.

The price was right—once again I only had to pay the maintenance charges—and it was spacious for a studio. But, being Parisian, it had its quirks. The inside of the front door was carpeted, presumably to keep the noise from bothering the neighbors. Considering my predilection for karaoke, I couldn't blame them. And the toilet had a wooden box built around it so that you could only see the seat, none of the mechanics. An ugly throne of sorts.

I invited Anne Marie over for drinks to christen the

place.

"It's quite large for a studio," she said.

"Yeah, surprisingly so. But the best part is there's a garbage chute right in the kitchen. You don't even have to get dressed!"

"I do always find that clothes get in the way of throwing away me trash," Anne Marie replied.

I had set myself up for that one. "Ha ha, very funny. You know what I mean. Normally you have to change out of your pajamas, throw on shoes, then go downstairs to throw out the trash. Now I'm free to throw it away whenever it suits me. Even in pajamas."

"Or naked."

"Fine, yes, naked. I throw my trash out naked. In fact, I'm always naked in my apartment and only just put on these clothes before you arrived."

"You better watch out for those windows, then."

The wall of windows offered a gorgeous view of the facing building and the lush garden nestled next to it. Grassy spaces are rare in big cities and here I had one right outside my window. During the day, the windows let in lots of sunshine. In the evening, they provided an unobstructed view to the neighbors across the way. Good thing I didn't actually walk around in the buff.

❧

When Chris had graciously offered her apartment, we agreed it would only be for three months. Enough time for me to get back on my post-break-up feet and decide whether or not I wanted to stay in France.

"Now you can go home!" people said, as if I had been a prisoner in the torturous city of Paris. Why did they think that? I loved it here, despite my complaints. I had chosen to come here on my own and found myself on my own once again. Why would I move back to the US just because

I broke up with my boyfriend? Paris was where I wanted to rest my feet.

But as spring rolled around, I needed a new apartment to rest them in.

I hunted on my favorite website—say it with me now—Craigslist, but didn't find any decent rentals. Anytime I'd stumble across a listing in my price range I would discover, upon further inspection, that the price quoted was the weekly rent, not monthly. Yowza. The apartments seemed geared more towards short-term stays, such as a job relocation or a season abroad. For a once-in-a-lifetime stay in Paris, 3,000€ per month might work for some people. But not for me.

Amazingly, I found an apartment right down the street from Chris's studio. In fact, it was back on my old street. The shady real estate agent (aren't they all?) photocopied a disturbing amount of my personal information, and in a matter of hours I held a new set of oddly shaped keys in my hands.

I crammed everything into my trusty old suitcases and rolled them back down the street. Once inside the building, five daunting flights of stairs greeted me.

These were no ordinary stairs.

They were designed by Satan and perfected by Death on his day off. The risers were the exact wrong height and required more than a normal amount of energy to mount them. And each flight had a few more steps than there should have been. The apartment didn't have luxuriously high ceilings, so the floors must have been three feet deep to compensate.

Taking a deep breath, I hauled one suitcase up the steps. Maybe someone would steal the other one so I wouldn't have to carry it. Descending the stairs, jeans clinging to my legs from sweat (sexy!), I found the damn thing still waiting for me in the lobby.

When I had moved out of Pierre's place, I left behind

the furniture we bought together. And as it had been winter, I left behind my upright fan.

I was now regretting the fan.

Seizing the excuse for a break, I collapsed on the steps and texted Pierre:

> Hey! Random question. Can I pick up fan?

He pinged back within seconds:

> Damn, hoping u forgot. Yep, u can pick up.

I felt funny going to his place as a guest when I had lived there for so long. As I rode up to the seventh floor in the world's tiniest elevator, I did a quick once-over in the mirror. I'd looked better, and definitely less sweaty, but it could have been worse.

I knocked on the door and held my breath. When Pierre answered, we paused awkwardly while deciding how to greet each other. We settled on *la bise*, which seemed formal and weird but I guess was appropriate.

"Good to see you." He seemed to genuinely mean it. "Come in."

My eyes darted around the apartment as I followed him in. Clearly a bachelor lived here now. More dirty dishes had piled up than I ever knew we owned. Papers were scattered everywhere. The apartment was almost a caricature, as if a set director had received instructions to make it look like a recently-broken up workaholic lived there. You had to *try* to make it that messy.

As a neat-freak, the state of his place was driving me crazy. As his ex-girlfriend, I was happy. This mess was no longer mine to worry about.

"How's work?" I asked.

"Busy as usual." He unplugged the fan and wrapped the cord around it. We had already run out of things to say, and it was just as well because the heat was rising in his apartment.

"Well, thanks," I said. "See you around."

"Yeah, see you," he said, as we gave *la bise* again. "Goodbye."

ॐ

The scene had been a bit weird but it reaffirmed, to both of us, that we'd made the right decision. Plus now I had a fan.

Hauling it down the street, I left a trail of sweat in my wake. For a city usually cold and gray, it sure picked an inopportune time for a sunny day.

I punched in my building's door code and saw my suitcase still waiting for me. Sigh. *Let's get this over with.*

As I clunked up the steps, I promised myself to never move again.

On the second floor landing I noticed an outlet on the wall. A light bulb went off in my head. I retrieved the fan and plugged it in. Ahh, relief.

My face buried in the breeze, I didn't hear the door from 2A open. "Bonjour, mademoiselle."

I prepared to explain myself but he just smiled and wished me a good afternoon.

After making it up the final three flights, I closed the door behind me and surveyed my new domain. I'd been in France for four years but this was the first apartment I could truly call my own. A new chapter of my life was about to begin.

But first, I needed to plug in my fan.

13

Not Before a Cup of Coffee, Honey

Now that I was single and in my new digs, it was time to take care of business. Though I'd been in Paris for several years, I'd managed to avoid a lot of bureaucracy involving proof of residency. Which was good at the time but sucked now.

Since my freelance work dropped US dollars into my American bank account, I didn't need a French account and I'd never had a French utility bill in my name. I didn't even have a mobile phone contract—my remote-control-sized contraption was on a pay-as-you-go plan.

And previously, while I'd stumbled through French conversations on a daily basis, I always knew in the back of my mind that Pierre could handle the tricky stuff for me (like, if the internet was out *again*).

But in order to pay my hefty rent on my own, I'd need a bank account. And if I didn't want the electricity to get shut off when the previous tenant's contract ran out, I needed to set up my own electricity. And if I wanted to write snarky blog posts about all of this, an internet connection might come in handy.

Before doing any of that, I needed to renew my visa. It wouldn't do much good to have lights and Wi-Fi if they deported me back to the US.

Life was so much more complicated here! I'd lived on my own for years in St. Louis and knew how to use a hammer and (call customer service to) fix the internet. I wasn't helpless, just a little less able to help myself in a foreign country.

I sighed. This was going to be rough. I had no choice but to go it alone. No boyfriend to help translate or carry the 400 sheets of paper required for the visa renewal appointment.

⌘

The blustery day of my appointment arrived and I made sure to show up five minutes early. Having murdered several forests of trees to print my dossier, I was as ready as I was ever going to be.

French bureaucracy really is as bad as you've heard.

Along with the renewal notice, the ever helpful government agents had included a list of ten items I needed to bring to my appointment. Here are the highlights:

Recent passport + 2 copies.
Easy. They give you a false sense of security by starting with the one thing that's not going to cause you trouble.

Three passport-sized photos.
Easy, but it's annoying that they only need three when the stupid machines force you to buy four. What am I going to do with the fourth picture? It's always the world's worst shot, anyway. (I can hear my mom saying now, "Oh

honey, I'm sure you look great in your photo!" Aren't moms the best? Maybe I can send my spare photo to her.)

Sitting in the photo booth, smiling at my own reflection, I attempted an expression so that on a scale of "might look OK in the dark" to "serial killer" I'd end up somewhere in the "frighten young children" range.

Birth certificate, dated no more than six months ago, translated, + 2 copies.

Why does it need to be dated no more than six months ago? I was born on the same date regardless of when the document is reissued. I have to renew the visa every year, yet I need a birth certificate less than six months old? That requires a continual cycle of requesting my birth certificate and submitting it for translation so that I'm always prepared for the next visa appointment. I'm a hamster on a wheel, minus the cardio workout.

Proof of residence, such as rent receipts or utility bills, for the past three months, + 2 copies.

Having just moved into my apartment, I didn't have three months' worth of rent receipts, nor did I have three months' worth of bills. I was scared.

Bank statements for the past three months, with a minimum balance, + 2 copies.

Even after suffering through the opening of a French bank account, I didn't have a sufficient number of account statements. And transferring money to meet the ever-so-specific "minimum balance" had proved to be a right pain. My American bank was as confused as my French bank, and each pointed their finger at the other saying that they needed to do blah blah blah.

Luckily, I found a brilliant way to bypass this. Each morning for a week, I withdrew the daily maximum from the ATM inside the bank branch. I could have used the outside ATM, but then the bank tellers wouldn't see my enormous eye roll. By using my American bank card, I pulled funds from my US account (plus hefty charges, yay!) and turned them into euros. Then I walked two steps over to the teller, filled out the deposit form, and waited for them to manually deposit the cash into my French bank account. Tedious? Yes. But it worked.

The bank teller printed off a statement-to-date, making me only 2 3/4 months shy of the required three months of bank statements. Maybe the visa renewal agent would be lenient?

I still had no idea what the required minimum balance was, but as I had money in my account, I technically had a minimum balance.

I entered the monochromatic waiting room and politely waited at the counter for the receptionist to arrive. It was 8:40 and my appointment time was 8:45. Right on schedule.

I drummed my fingers on the counter as the minutes ticked by. Where was the receptionist? The *Préfecture* opened at 8:30, so she should have been there by now. How would she check everyone in on time for their appointments?

Silly me, I forgot that employees get their coffee first and then give kisses to everyone in the office.

"Bonjour, Sandrine! Comment s'est passé ton week-end?" Jocelyne the Mean Government Worker would ask.

"Très bien, Jocelyne. Et toi?" Sandrine the Equally Mean Government Worker would respond, kissing each of Jocelyne's cheeks.

I'm fine with that relaxed approach to starting your day, but it should be done before employees are on the clock. You couldn't possibly call what they're doing "work" so it shouldn't be done during work hours. Why should I have to wait while they drink their coffee and chit-chat, thus making me late for my appointment?

Of course, the person I had an appointment with, Pauline, was also getting coffee and giving kisses so there was no way I'd be taken in at 8:45 anyway.

I continued to patiently wait for the receptionist since the sign on her desk said to wait patiently for the receptionist. The sign also said to have all necessary papers out and ready. Done.

However, I knew there'd be trouble the moment I spotted a stupid girl sitting in the front row of seats with her stupid mom. We'll call them Bitch and Bitch's Mom.

They had gotten there before me so I knew Bitch was going to butt in front of me in line. Sorry, but just because you arrive first doesn't mean you get to be first in line— stand up and serve your time like the rest of us! Obviously we all want to relax in a chair instead of standing in line while Jocelyne and Sandrine and Pauline blather on about their weekends. But that's not how it works. Jocelyne and Sandrine and Pauline kiss and chat and sip coffee while we wait with fake smiles on our faces hoping they approve our visas without hassle. We don't ignore signs and we don't sit on chairs.

To be sure I wasn't being unrightfully mean, I checked to make sure Bitch didn't have a cane or some other legitimate reason for not standing in line. I also checked to see if perhaps she left her stack of papers on the receptionist's desk, as a weak attempt to save her place in line.

Nope, nothing. Just pure bitch, assuming we'd hold her place in line. I shot her a look that said "That's not happening, honey. Get up here and wait with the rest of us." It was a long look.

She seemed to pick up what I was putting down so she heaved her lazy ass up, sauntered over, and declared, "I was first in line." Oh, honey, you don't know how right you are! "Was" is the operative word here. I *was* thinner in high school. I *was* a big fan of Vanilla Ice. But these are in the past. I *am* now at the front of the line. I *am* standing and waiting patiently like the sign told me to. Well, maybe not patiently. But I'm standing and that should count for something.

Of course I didn't say any of this. The most I could muster was, "I get it. I'm still gonna keep my shit on the counter and stand here." Take *that*! I totally wimped out but getting in a fight right before my appointment probably wouldn't help Pauline's decision to let me stay in the country.

I peeked at the clock. 8:50. *How much longer is this going to take?* At least now Bitch was firmly planted in front of me and I didn't have to worry about any last-minute surprise attacks. Maybe I could endure the rest of my wait in peace.

"Vous êtes Américaine?" someone behind me with an American accent asked.

Guessing she was talking to me, I turned to reply and bumped right into her face. Geez, was she close enough? I took a step back, not needing to be any nearer to her graying rat's nest of hair.

And what a stupid question. My American passport was in plain sight and I had spoken in English. Short of waving the flag and belting out "The Star Spangled Banner" (though if I had to wait any longer, I might have), it was pretty obvious I was American.

"Yes," I replied, turning back to the front of the line.

Not deterred, she continued. "Moi aussi."

Moi au-freaking-ssi? She just said she was American! Why was she speaking to me in French? It's probably an irrational pet peeve of mine but I hate that. Like, was she practicing her French? With an American? There are way better people to practice with. Or was she showing off? Because I wasn't impressed. Even my mom can say "Me too" in French. Or was she simply a nice human being making conversation? Well? Well? Well. Ahem. That was probably it. But it was still annoying. After the Battle of Bitch I didn't have the energy to make small talk with some weirdo.

And, geez, could Jocelyne and Sandrine and Pauline *please* wrap it up? I didn't know how much longer I could keep my cool, if you could even call it cool anymore.

ॐॐ

After finally checking in, I was given a number and told to wait in the chairs where Bitch and Bitch's Mom were comfortably installed. Great, more waiting. At least Rat's Nest found a spot on the other side of the room.

An eternity later, my number was called. I strode confidently to the *guichet* (any relation to the guillotine?), the desk where Pauline, the unsmiling bureaucrat handling my case today, was waiting for me.

"Bonjour," I said, with a medium-caliber smile. You don't want to smile too much or they'll think you're covering up your lack of proper documents. But you have to give some sort of a smile or they'll hate you and will overly scrutinize your documents.

"Bonjour," she reluctantly replied. The French observe niceties, even if it kills them.

She grabbed my dossier. Passport plus copies—check. So far so good. Then she picked up the photos, frowning. "You're smiling in the photos."

"That way you know it's me!" I said with a smile. It didn't go over as well as I'd hoped.

"You can't smile in official photos."

Crap! Would this ruin the entire appointment before we'd even gotten started?

"But we'll let it slide this time. Next time, though," she said, pointing a stern finger at me, "don't smile."

I promised her I wouldn't. But I didn't mean it. Clearly she has the power to let smiling photographs slide through the system, so I would take my chances next time, too. It's a risk, but it's better than having a serial killer mug shot.

The birth certificate was approved with no problem. Which is good since I'd paid nearly $200 to issue it, expedite its delivery to France, and have it translated by an approved official translator.

Pauline the Mean was gruff, but we were getting through this about on par with the pain of ripping off a band-aid—that is, painful but mercifully quick.

I even survived the lack of utility bills and rent receipts snafu by explaining that I had recently broken up with my boyfriend, and moved out on my own and thus only had my first month's worth of papers to show. I had wisely brought all my previous documents to show that I had lived *somewhere*, which she seemed to appreciate even though I can't imagine what it proves.

Then we got to the bank statements.

Here I finally learned the required minimum balance (though it would have been infinitely more helpful if it had been indicated on the renewal notice). When I'd previously been "hosted" by Pierre, the state wasn't too concerned about my finances since he was accountable for me. But now that I was on my own, I had to maintain a minimum balance of "mille deux." This translates to "thousand-two" so understandably I was confused. 1002 euros? That seems odd. But if she meant 2000 then shouldn't she have said "deux mille?" If she meant 1200 then it seems she should have said "douze cent" (twelve hundred) or "mille deux cent" (one thousand two hundred).

"Mille deux?" I asked.

"Oui," she replied, as if I was dumb. Which I was because by posing the same question back to her, I'd only confirmed that my ears work, not that I understood what she meant.

"OK, deux mille," I tried. "Et c'est pour l'année?" Did I need to keep that amount in the bank for a whole year?

"Non, MILLE DEUX. Et c'est par mois. Multipliez le montant par 12 et laissez-le sur votre compte en banque toute l'année." No, it's whatever-the-hell mille deux is. And it's per month. So multiply it by 12 and keep it in your bank account all year.

Hold the phone. What? First, I wish *she* would have multiplied it by 12 because then perhaps I could have gotten clarification on this whole mille deux business. Second, I have to keep that money in the bank and not use it? So that means I need extra money on top of that for rent and utilities? I don't know many people who can afford to keep 14,400€ (assuming that was even the right number) in the bank all year without touching it.

"That's expensive," I said.

"Well, Paris is expensive, honey. Deposit the money and come back to see me."

She kind of missed my point. I understand that Paris is expensive and I could easily spend that much money each month. But to spend that much on top of keeping an equal amount in the bank seemed unreal. I hoped that maybe I had just misunderstood but I couldn't figure out how to ask the right question.

Pauline slid my dossier across the table to me. Meeting over. I would have liked for her to review my other papers so I'd know what else I'd screwed up but she was already on her way to the coffee machine. Better luck next time.

Eventually I got all my documents together and was the proud owner of a long-stay tourist visa with my own address on the back[10]. I'd been legal the past few years but

---

[10] And with mille-deux-times-12 euros in the bank. Pauline the Mean never did explain what she meant, so I took a wild guess it was 1200 euros, then painstakingly transferred funds into my account, never to be touched again. At least I had a getaway fund if I ever decided to

my documentation had been done alongside Pierre's name. This was the first card that was all mine! A lot of sweat and tears (and paper cuts) went into that tiny card. It was my most prized possession.

---

leave this gloriously bureaucratic country.

14

The Christening

My new apartment (mine!) was miniscule. But it had its advantages. Less surface area to clean. I didn't need to buy a couch because there wasn't any place to put it. And I could cook and work at the same time.

The kitchen table doubled as my work station, which was within arm's reach of the stove, microwave, and refrigerator. Need to stir the omelet? No problem! Top off your cup of coffee? Coming right up. No need to even get out of your chair!

Nestled against the petite bedroom was the petite bathroom, which came in handy my first night there.

"Hey there!" Anne Marie had invited me to a bar opening in the 16th *arrondissement*. It was part of a chain of microbreweries dotted throughout Paris, so beer featured prominently on their menu. "All beer and drinks that contain beer are free tonight."

"Drinks that contain beer? Like, beer…cocktails?" I'd never heard of that before. Weird.

"Yeah, weird huh? But you get more alcohol that way. I'm drinking a Long Island Iced Beer. My stomach is going to make me pay for it later."

Anne Marie had a stomach of steel so if she thought this was rough, I should have taken notice. But as I was perpetually on a budget, I wanted to maximize any free alcohol at my disposal. I perused the "Beer Cocktails" section of the menu.

"I'll have a Beergarita," I ordered, slightly gagging.

It tasted surprisingly OK, and I got a few down the hatch before moving on to Beermopolitans.

"I heard in Iceland they add shots to their beer to make it stronger," I said to Anne Marie. "The government tried to reduce alcoholism by lowering the alcohol content of beer so that's how they make up for it."

"Sounds like their plan didn't work, unless everyone vomits before they get drunk."

"Ugh, let's stop talking about it before I throw up."

"Good call. So, have you heard the new Kylie album?"

Despite the change in topic, it was too late. My woozy stomach told me I needed to get home and quick. It was only midnight, making it an embarrassingly early time to be leaving a party with free drinks but all the hidden alcohol in those nasty cocktails had caught up with me.

I pulled an Irish goodbye[11] and bolted out of there. At

---

[11] For those who don't know, an Irish goodbye is what it's called when you leave without saying goodbye to anyone. The best way I've found to pull it off is to say you're going to the bathroom or outside to make a phone call, but then just never come back. Although that presumes you have a choice in the matter. Plenty of people just drunkenly stumble out the door without realizing they haven't said goodbye. Interestingly, the French call it an English goodbye and Germans call it a French goodbye. Clearly, except for the Irish, we all like to blame other people for our inability to leave politely.

least I didn't leave Ammo with my tab since my drinks had been free. I remember taking a taxi home but the rest was a blur.

༉༘

I woke up shivering. Looking around, I tried to get my bearings. Where the heck was I?

A toilet and a shower. Ew. Clearly I'd been sleeping on a bathroom floor. I rubbed my eyes and took another look around. *No, seriously, where the heck am I?*

My foot touched something soft and squishy. I sat up and dared to inspect it. *Ah, there we go. My bed.* I'd been at home. I hadn't recognized it since I'd only moved in the day before and had essentially been drinking ever since. Ahem.

My cell phone buzzed, the sound muffled from being buried at the bottom of my purse. Why is your phone always at the bottom of your purse?

I rummaged in my bag as frantically as my dizzy head could manage and answered the call just before it could head to voice mail. "Hello?"

"Hi stranger." Anne Marie's voice was way too chipper for this time of day.

"Why are you calling so early?" I snapped.

"Early? It's 11:00. And that's the thanks I get for checking in on a friend? Geez."

"Sorry. My head is pounding and apparently I slept on the bathroom floor. Well halfway in the bathroom, halfway in the bedroom. That makes it somewhat better, right?"

"Ha, if you say so. I guess you got home OK? I was worried after you pulled the ol' Irish goodbye."

"You guys call them that, too?"

"Hey, us Irish, we know what we're like. We call a spade a spade. Anyway, I warned you those beer cocktails were bad news."

"And one of these days I'm going to listen to you. In the meantime, I'm going to bed. It's about time."

15

The Popcorn Incident

One gray Sunday, Anne Marie suggested we go to a movie with Wooster. I took the Métro to Cour St. Emilion, a quaint cobblestoned *quartier* that used to be a train station but now housed dozens of trendy restaurants and shops, plus a giant movie theater.

We were slated to see *The Hangover*, or *Very Bad Trip* as it's bizarrely called in "French." You see, the French often translate American movie titles from English into... English. It's weird. I mean, I get it—the original title is just confusing enough that the typical French person (who shouldn't be expected to know English) won't understand. But then why not translate it into, dare I even suggest it, French?

I hear you asking for some examples. Without further ado, here's a short list of "French" movie titles, but fear not—there are plenty more where these came from:

1. Very Bad Trip (originally The Hangover)

2. Very Bad Cops (originally The Other Guys)

3. Happiness Therapy (originally Silver Linings Playbook)

4. Happy New Year (originally New Year's Eve)

5. Sex List (originally What's Your Number?)

6. Sex Academy (originally Not Another Teen Movie)

7. Sex Friends (originally No Strings Attached)

8. Sex Crimes (originally Wild Things)

9. Sexe Intentions (originally Cruel Intentions)

10. Crazy Night (originally Date Night)

11. In The Air (originally Up In The Air)

12. Night and Day (originally Knight and Day)

13. American Boys (originally Varsity Blues)

Notice a few themes? In case you plan to apply for the dream job of translating English movie titles into English for French audiences, here are the only rules you need to follow:

1. Remove any extra prepositions

2. Strip out any plays on words—we don't want to have any fun here!

3. When in doubt, add the word "sex". Everything's better with sex in it.

Now that we understand the French movie title system, let's return to our regularly scheduled programming. Where was I? Oh yes, *Very Bad Trip.*

The movie was playing at 12:45, so we had rushed to meet at the theater by 12:30. By the time we made it to the front of the line, it was 12:35. Whew, we still had time.

"Trois places pour Very Bad Trip," Wooster ordered. Ammo and I snickered as she said "Very Bad Trip" with a French accent, so that it sounded like "Verrrr-ee Bad-uh Treeep." As if it wasn't very bad enough she had to say the stupid Frenchified title, she had to say it with a French accent in order to be understood.

The cashier handed her the tickets as we scurried to the popcorn stand. Time was ticking!

We ordered three popcorns and, an insane amount of money later, were ready to see the movie. Wooster handed the ticket-stub-ripper guy our tickets.

"Quatrième salle à gauche," he said. Fourth room on the left. "Hold on. These tickets are for later. You can go wait over there," he said, indicating a wooden bench.

The three of us simultaneously raised our eyebrows. Why were our tickets for the later show? We still had two minutes before this show started! We already had popcorn! And he was insane if he thought we were going to sit on a bench for the next two hours.

After five minutes of polite but firm back and forth, Wooster made a deal with Ticket Ripper. He would take our popcorn back and give us a note saying we had already paid for three popcorns, which we could collect before our show. It wasn't ideal—we still had two hours to kill—but at least we didn't have to carry our popcorn around with us or eat it on a stupid bench. We nodded our consent and he dashed off with our popcorn.

"That's all fine and well, yeah, but you know we're getting the SAME popcorns back, yeah?" Anne Marie pointed out.

She was right. Ticket Ripper had squished our popcorns up against the side of the popcorn machine, smushing them beyond recognition. Great, now we'd have stale, crummy popcorn that would slip out the sides of the destroyed containers.

Ticket Ripper came back with a scrap of paper with "3 popcorn" scrawled on it.

"I doubt handing over this piece of paper in two hours is going to result in us getting three popcorns," I said to the girls.

"I know! Anyone could have written this note," Wooster said. "And this guy might not even be here when we come back."

"And this whole thing shouldn't have even happened anyway! We were on time for the 12:45 show," Ammo said.

Of course, the quickest way to get over frustration like this is a glass of wine. Hoping for the best, we headed to a café and passed the next couple of hours over some rosé. I could think of worse ways to pass the time.

At 2:40, we returned to the movie theater with a light buzz and a huge appetite. And believe it or not, when we handed our paper over to the popcorn guy, Ticket Ripper gave a subtle nod of assent, making us the proud owners of three shiny, new cartons of popcorn.

A modern day miracle! We were ecstatic. Maybe it was the wine, maybe it was the surprisingly easy resolution, maybe we were just excited to stare at Bradley Cooper for the next two hours.

Oh, who am I kidding? It was definitely because of Bradley Cooper.

16

Movin' On Up

"You might want to sit down for this," Anne Marie said. "Next week I start work at a new bar. Tonight's me last night here."

Given that I'd pretty much single-handedly kept the bar in business, I felt as if I'd had the rug (or bar stool) pulled out from under me. "I'm gonna need another glass of wine," I said, while I processed the information.

The obvious solution was to go to her new place of employment, but it wasn't quite that easy. First, The Fifth Bar was in the part of town where my other favorite bars were. It was on the Rive Gauche, the Left Bank, which is the side of the river that people who live there think is better. The new place seemed worlds away, over on the other side of the Seine. How could I hit up all my regular haunts in the same night?

Second, her new bar was far from the grungy, worn,

comfortable pub I was used to. It was a private club for Swedish and Norwegian expats, though all nationalities were welcome to join. The club held private events for its members most nights, including occasional visits from Scandinavian royalty. It was only open to the public on Wednesday nights, where it held a Happy Hour/Open House. The whole concept was intimidating but piqued my curiosity.

Well, if I can move across an ocean, surely I can cross a river.

I took the plunge one warm Wednesday evening. Wearing a girly sleeveless shirt, snug jeans, and low heels, I buzzed the button for the Swedish Society, situated along one of Paris's grandest streets, rue de Rivoli. I pushed the heavy wooden door, opening onto a cobbled courtyard with luxury cars parked in it.

How did those get in here?

I turned back to the double doors and saw that if you were to open both doors, there would be enough room for a Jaguar to slide through. Who would have thought?

Now I had to find the actual club. Not this again! Three different staircases created who-knows-how-many possibilities. I chose the grandest of them, treading lightly on the lushly carpeted stairs. I slowed on the first level landing, but as there was only one apartment, without so much as a nameplate, I hedged my bets on the next floor.

Bingo! A gold plaque indicated I was in the right place. I rang the doorbell and a tough-looking black guy in a sharp suit opened the door. Yeah, this was definitely different from my usual scene. But after all these years in Paris, it was about time I hung out at a top-notch venue!

And what a place! The entry was the size of my apartment. A bright chandelier hung from an impossibly high ceiling. Scandinavian art adorned the walls and a marble side table displayed pictures of Princess Victoria of Sweden. Nice name.

Three rooms branched off the entryway, and as the bouncer sensed I had no idea where to go, he indicated which room the bar was in.

As my heels dug into a rug that surely cost more than my annual salary, I headed to the bar.

"Ah, you made it!" Ammo bellowed from behind the bar.

I slid into a barstool and gave the room a once-over. "Feels like I'm in a rich person's apartment."

"I know, right? What'll you have?"

"A glass of champagne[12] seems appropriate. So, how's work?"

We chatted as I sipped my bubbly. While it was pretty much the exact opposite of our former hangout, I still felt instantly at home.

"Hej. Hur mår du?" a tall girl with long blonde hair asked Anne Marie.

"Jag är bra, takk," she replied with her famous smile. From the sounds of it, they'd done the old "how-are-you-I'm-fine" bit in Swedish. I was impressed. Well, not by the blonde girl because she was obviously Swedish. But I was impressed Anne Marie had already picked up some useful phrases. I usually only picked up swear words in other languages.

"Vicki, this is Nina," Ammo said, as she poured the Swede a shot of Jack Daniels before she even asked. It put hair on my chest just looking at the liquor. Glancing at my glass of champagne, I felt comparatively dainty.

---

[12] Technically Champagne should be capitalized and should only be used when referring to the sparkling wine that comes from the Champagne region of France. I even signed an online petition years ago promising to follow those rules and now here I am breaking them. But to this American, it just seems snooty to capitalize Champagne so throughout the rest of the book please forgive me for not capitalizing it. And if you're the owner of the website with the petition, you can go ahead and slap my wrists.

"Hello!" I said. If she drank shots of Jack like they were nothing, clearly she wasn't uptight. This venue and its clientele fascinated me.

"Well, I'd love to stay and chat but I need to go earn me salary," Anne Marie said as she left us to help other customers.

"Have you seen the rest of the club? I'll show you around," Nina offered.

The rest of the venue was even more impressive. A modern room with stark Scandinavian furniture was followed by the Grand Salon with a grand piano and several cozy two-person tables. A boardroom housed a desk that at one time belonged to famed Swede Alfred Nobel. The final room on the tour blended antique and modern, with a splash of 20th century Swedish art on its deep red walls.

The place was huge!

We headed back through the Grand Salon to a balcony that ran the length of the building. The balcony offered an unobstructed view of the Louvre and the Tuileries Gardens. The massive clock on the Musée d'Orsay peeked through branches of the Jardin de Tuileries, and the Eiffel Tower scraped the sky in the distance. If you leaned forward (but not far enough to fall and knock out your two front teeth), you could see the Arc de Triomphe at the end of the Champs Elysées.

Not too shabby.

After tipping back the last of my champagne, we headed back to the bar.

"Nice, huh?" Anne Marie asked.

"Yeah, I could get used to this," I replied. I don't know what I'd been so afraid of. I guess I'd thought it would be too fancy and that I'd feel out of place.

"I'll have another shot, *takk*," Nina said.

No worries, there. I was right at home.

17

The Belle of the Ball

A perk of hanging out in highfalutin places like the Swedish Society was that I heard about other highfalutin places. Such as a charity ball to raise funds for an Irish organization. Good cause, free drinks, a primarily English-speaking crowd. Sold!

Also, as I'd now been single for quite some time, I hoped to meet a handsome guy at the ball. How romantic would that be? We'd dance the night away, maybe I'd lose a glass slipper and...

Nina snapped me out of my reverie. "So we're going to the ball?"

"You bet!" I was ready to slip my dancing shoes on and party in style.

ॐ∼ॐ

The night of the ball, we got ready in my apartment

over a couple of bottles of champagne. We were flush with anticipation of the night ahead. After downing the last glass, we tottered down the five flights of stairs in too-high heels. Screw the Métro, we were taking a cab.

As the taxi stopped in front of the hotel, we jumped out. The night begins!

The ball was held on an upper floor of the hotel, with a grand balcony and even grander view. Drinks were cold and plentiful, and the ambiance was elegant with a paradoxical casual air about it. Just my speed.

"Hey there, stranger!"

I turned to see Chris and her husband, Dave. "Well, hello there! Fancy meeting you here," I said, kissing each of them on the cheek.

"We've actually run into a few other people as well. Reminds me just how small the English-speaking world in Paris is," Chris said.

"And how much we all like to drink!" Dave added. We all laughed.

"Well, we'll let you youngsters get on with it," Chris said. "Maybe we'll run into you later?"

Nina and I headed to the bar for champagne, then found our assigned table. After the slightly-too-long sit-down dinner and charity auction, the band finally started playing. The moment I'd been waiting for! I'm a horrific dancer, but the point of a ball is to dance. And meet a charming man.

We took to the floor and danced in the typical group-of-girls way—shaking your booty and throwing your hands in the air. Nothing if not classy.

A few songs in, a young Irish guy approached us. "Would you like to dance?" he asked me.

I swooned. He chose *me* out of all the girls! Having never been asked to dance at my high school dances, I was ecstatic. "Of course," I replied, trying to contain my glee.

And we were off. The band played big-band tunes

while my Irish lad flung me around the dance floor. He was smooth and easily compensated for my missteps (which were about every other one). I dizzily watched my emerald green dress twirl as we changed rhythm for a new song. I'd had just the right amount to drink to be uninhibited in my dance moves without being so tipsy that I'd fall over.

I was too out of breath to talk much (that's a first) but I did manage to ask his age.

"Nineteen," he boasted, a lock of hair falling in his boyish face.

Man, he was even younger than he looked. Yowza. Nineteen was a tad too young for this late-twenties girl. But no reason we couldn't dance the night away!

After what felt like fifty songs, I needed a break. I walked to the bar for a champagne refill and realized my feet were killing me. I'd been so caught up with swirling and twirling that I didn't notice my swollen feet rubbing against my now too-tight high heels.

"I'll have another glass of champagne, please," Nina said from behind me. "Having fun dancing with your teenager?"

"Can you believe it? He's so *young*. I'm surprised he's allowed to stay out this late!"

"You better get in a few more dances before his parents take him home."

"No way," I replied. "These feet are done dancing. In fact, they're done standing. I need to sit down. Catch you in a bit?"

I headed to our dinner table and fell into a chair. Much better. Though it would be even better if I could put my feet up.

Darting a look around to be sure no one was watching, I slid a chair over and rested my legs on it. My feet dangled off the edge so that my shoes weren't touching the seat of the chair. I may have been exhausted but I still had some semblance of manners.

I sipped my champagne and took in the scene. Aside from my worn-out feet, I felt great. I'd had a wonderful evening and danced more than I'd ever danced in my life. I should really go to balls more often.

Lost in thought, I didn't notice a gray-haired man saunter up. He pointed at my legs and made a face.

"Pardon, monsieur, mais c'est juste mes jambes qui sont sur la chaise, pas mes pieds." I clarified that it was just my legs on the chair, not my feet, hoping this would make him go away.

"No, no," he replied in English with an Irish accent. "I'm not worried about that. I was wondering if I could sit down."

Everyone was on the dance floor, leaving hundreds of empty seats at the dining tables, and he wanted to sit in *this* chair? The very one my tired legs were relaxing on? That probably meant he wanted to chat me up.

Oh well, it couldn't hurt to talk to him, right?

I slid my legs off the chair and he sat down. "You can put your legs back on the chair now," he said, as he grabbed one leg, slid off my shoe and started rubbing my foot.

What the heck just happened?

In one quick motion he had gone from kinda weird old dude to super weird old dude who was rubbing my foot.

I should stop this. Really. But damn that feels good. The whole reason I'd taken a break was because my feet were killing me, and now I had a free, albeit creepy, masseur. I told myself I'd just let him do it a little longer.

I sipped my champagne and looked straight ahead. Hopefully no one would spot us or I'd die of embarrassment. Or maybe not. Was it really that bad? On second thought, don't answer that.

After a while, he finished the first foot. I had been so relaxed that the abrupt stop came as a shock. Part of me was glad the awkwardness was over, but part of me felt like the other foot needed a little rubby-rub. I mean, we should probably even it out.

He must have read my expression, whipping my left leg into position as he began massaging circles into the arch of my foot. Creepiness never felt so good.

I leaned back and let myself enjoy it. The champagne had blurred my judgment and this didn't even seem that bad anymore. Just a guy rubbing a girl's feet. Who he had just met. OK, yeah, there wasn't a good way to spin it. But my aching feet didn't care.

I zoned out, listened as the band played another song, and sipped what remained of my champagne. I reached the bottom of my glass and looked up, then noticed things had started to get weird. Well, they had *started* to get weird the minute this guy sat down. Perhaps I should say things had started to get weird enough that I had to end it.

You see, Mr. Foot Fetish had removed his necktie and was rubbing it back and forth in a saw-like motion between my big toe and the toe next to it[13]. What is that? Is that a thing? Do people do that? And do other people let them, aside from tipsy girls at charity galas with tired feet? Does he come to this event every year and wait in the shadows, scoping out his target?

No matter how his operation worked, I needed out. It'd have been bad enough if someone caught us while he was providing a much-needed massage. But to be caught in the act of tie-toe dry humping, well, that would be hard to recover from.

"Thank you sir, but I must be getting back to my friends," I stammered as I stood up. I wobbled as I

---

[13] Is it called your pointer toe, like how the finger closest to your thumb is your pointer finger? It doesn't do much pointing. Or is it called your index toe, since the pointer finger can also be called an index finger? Or does it have a different name entirely? If I didn't spend so much time letting old men rub my toes, I might have time to find out.

crammed my feet into my heels. Thank you? Who thanks a guy who molested her foot? There's a question I never thought I'd ask.

He smiled and said, "Anytime."

Oh dear God, I hope not. I dashed to the bar, where thankfully (and unsurprisingly) I ran into Nina again.

"Where've you been?" she asked.

"You don't want to know," I replied as I tried to make eye contact with the bartender.

"Well I do *now!*" she shouted as the bartender came over.

"A glass of champagne, please," I ordered. "Oh, who are we kidding? Two." I watched the bubbly fill the glasses, only breaking my silence once I had two flutes of forgetful-juice in hand. "Let's just say my toes lost their virginity to that old creep over there."

"Who? That guy who's waving at you?"

I looked over and sure enough, my new boyfriend was smiling and waving at me. Oh the shame. This was about as far away from a Cinderella fairy tale as you could get. Leave it to me to go to a ball in Paris and instead of a charming man chasing after me with a glass slipper, I got toe-humped by a creepster. At least the free champagne helped wash it all away.

The sun shone brightly in my eyes, waking me up the next morning long before I was ready. I had consumed way too much champagne the night before. And muscles I previously never knew existed now ached.

But my feet felt great.

I dragged myself out of bed, tripping over my shoes as I headed to the bathroom. As my eyes fell on the offending objects, memories of the previous night flooded back to me. How utterly embarrassing!

Staring in the bathroom mirror I saw two tired, yet vibrantly green, eyes staring back at me. "Vicki, don't give up! Yes, creepy old men like you, but a normal guy will, too."

I declared then and there that this was the summer I'd find a new guy, an awesome guy, a guy old enough to not have a curfew but not so old that he was on a pension.

While I may not have *needed* a man, I had to admit I wanted one.

18

Wankers That You Meet In Bars

"Your problem is you go for the wrong guys," Ammo said as we relaxed over a bottle of wine. We shaded ourselves from the afternoon sun under the immense awning of a sidewalk café in the Marais.

"And which guys are those?" Maybe she had some insight.

"Wankers that you meet in bars. And English-speaking bars at that. Those lot are only looking for a one-night stand with an easy American girl."

I topped up our glasses, then returned the bottle to the ice bucket. She was right. A few months had passed since the infamous ball and I was no closer to finding Prince Charming. I'd spent the summer bar-hopping on my usual circuit, talking to guys who always turned out to be jerks or already had girlfriends or both. It was tiring.

But how else was I supposed to meet someone? I worked from home, exercised at an all-female gym, and volunteered for an organization where the membership veered toward the older end of the spectrum. All my remaining time was spent in English pubs.

"So what should I do?"

"Oh I dunno. But not what you're doing."

"Gee, thanks." Not helpful. "I always read in magazines that you should stop thinking about it and then it will happen. But that's not really me. I overanalyze everything so of course I'm going to think about this."

"I'm not sure what kind of magazines you're reading but I guess I agree. Just chill. It's not like you need to meet someone tonight."

❧

Inspired by Anne Marie's wine-induced words of wisdom, I went out for Girl's Night at The Long Hop. Determined *not* to meet a guy, I had gone makeup-free (not that I ever wore much) and was dressed simply in a strapless blue summery top and my trusty, old form-fitting jeans.

I alternated between drinking at the bar and busting moves on the dance floor. I truly wasn't even thinking about guys. I was only thinking about having fun with the girls and not puking after taking Jägerbomb shots.

But as they say, the best laid plans...

"I'm gonna get another drink," I shouted to Nina as I wove my way through the throng of sweaty people on the dance floor.

I set my glass on the bar and searched for a menu. Normally I drank wine, but I was in the mood for something different. It was hot and I wanted a cool drink, but I didn't often venture into cocktail territory for fear that it would have one ice cube and weird mixers (which is what had happened nearly every other time I'd ordered an overpriced cocktail in France).

I spotted the cocktail board on the wall behind the bar. There we go. A margarita could be good. Or did I want a beer? I glanced at the options on the beer taps to help make the important decision.

And that's when I noticed the tall, gorgeous guy standing next to the beer taps. In spite of myself, my mind formed a plan.

Edging over to him, I decided to ask his advice. I'd said I wasn't looking for a guy and I wasn't, I swear. I was just going to ask his opinion on what to order.

"Hey," I began.

The tanned stranger turned to me with a surprised expression, but answered with a polite "Hello."

"Can you help me? I can't decide between a beer and a margarita."

He hesitated.

"I'll pay," I quickly threw in. "I'm only looking for some advice." I didn't want him to think this was some sneaky way of getting him to buy me a drink. It was just my sneaky way of striking up a conversation.

"Well, beer is always a safe bet," he said in perfect but accented English. "You can't go wrong. But a margarita could be a nice change. I heard they're good here. Plus it's hot out so that would probably be refreshing. Then again, so is a cold beer. Umm..."

How cute was that? He took my question seriously, as if lives depended on which concoction I imbibed. "Now you see my problem. Both sound good. But which one sounds better?"

"I'd have to say beer. But I'm a guy and I always drink beer."

"OK, Beer Drinking Guy, thank you for your help," I said with a smile. I leaned over the counter and made eye contact with the bartender. "I'll have a pint of lager, please." I turned back to my new friend.

"My name is Mika. Nice to meet you," he said.

"Vicki. Nice to meet you too."

"You are American?" he asked. "Where from?"

"St. Louis," I answered, cringing as I waited for him to say "Louisiana."

"That's in Missouri, right? You have the Rams for American football, the Blues for hockey, and you don't have a basketball team, unless you count the college team, the, uh, what are they called?"

Amazed he knew my hometown so well, I happily helped him out. "The Billikens. St. Louisans are allowed to cheer for the Chicago Bulls since we don't have our own professional basketball team but I'll slap you if you say you're a fan of any other Chicago team, particularly the Cubs."

"Ha, don't worry. I don't like the Cubs. Or the White Sox for that matter." He winked as he took a gulp of his beer.

I liked this guy. Too bad I'd told myself I wasn't looking for a relationship.

∽✤∾

Mika and I chatted until the Long Hop closed.

"You crack me up," he said. "I'm having a really good time."

"Me too!" This was how it should be! Not only were we having a blast, but he wasn't afraid to say it. Points for honesty.

Of course, the real test would be how the night ended. Would he ask for my number and then barrage me with over-the-top text messages? Would he try to get me in bed and then call me a *salope* (Mom, don't look up what that word means) when I refused? Would he take my digits and then never call? Because these were all the wonderful scenarios that had burned me out on the dating scene.

The dating scene that I had just sworn off of.

Yikes, what was I doing? And with a French guy nonetheless. I really was asking for it.

"Well, I should go home. I'm helping a friend move tomorrow morning. Can we meet up tomorrow afternoon?" he asked, his eyebrows raised as if he wasn't sure I would say yes. Points for not being cocky.

I hadn't considered this possibility. A nice guy ending the night on a nice note and already planning a future date? I could still be in for 42 text messages but it was worth the risk. "Sounds great! How about we meet at the St. Michel fountain at, say, 4:00?"

"Cool. That should give me enough time to finish moving my friend's stuff. See you then," he said with a smile, then winked before walking towards the Métro. Points for not trying to get me in bed.

It was getting hard to keep track of all his points.

ভত্ত

The next day I was more excited than I wanted to admit. I was supposed to be guy-free and here I had a date. A date! I hadn't had a proper one of those in a long time. What to wear? What to do? What to say?

Since it was a hot summer day, I settled on a flirty sleeveless shirt with jeans and flip flops. Casual but pretty, comfortable but not slobby. Too casual for a date with a French guy? I guess we'd find out.

I hopped on the Métro and arrived at St. Michel right at 4:00. Dork! I slipped on my sunglasses as I made my way over to the fountain and looked around for my date.

What if I didn't recognize him? I'd had quite a few drinks the night before. Or what if he didn't recognize me? Or what if I did recognize him but he wasn't nearly as attractive as I remembered? Or, gasp, what if I wasn't as attractive as he remembered and he ran away?

I looked up to see if anyone was running away. Right

then, I saw a tall guy with slightly messy dark hair emerge from the Métro, smiling in my direction.

Ahem. He did show up after all, with bonus points for being on time. And the spring in his step meant he still thought I was good-looking, or else had bad vision.

"Hello," he said, shyly.

"Hi," I nearly shouted back. Whoa, tone it down. Was I nervous?

He leaned in to give *la bise*, one kiss on each cheek, which seemed formal for a date but then what else are you supposed to do? We're not going to make out in the street, but it would be weird to not greet each other at all (well, not weird in America but definitely weird in France. Where we presently were. Let's get back to it.)

"I was thinking maybe we could walk toward Île St. Louis and get ice cream at Berthillon?" he proposed.

I was thinking I love you already. Ice cream—yippee! Keep it cool. "That sounds great."

We strolled along the Seine toward the small island. My stomach fluttered. A real date with a real Frenchman doing real Frenchie stuff! Wheeeeee!

༄

The date continued as the sun began to set. We walked along rue de Rivoli, talking about anything and everything. We stopped in an Irish bar where I knew a few people (making me look cool). Then we headed to Fête de Tuileries, the yearly summer carnival held in the Tuileries Gardens.

"Ooh! Check out that booth!" I shouted, as I dashed across the dusty gravel to a stand where you could shoot balloons with BBs. "I'm pretty good at this," I said, dropping my money on the counter and picking up a rifle. "Watch."

Showing off my marksmanship, I obliterated the

balloons. They never stood a chance. As I claimed my prize, I noticed Mika's mixed expression. He was impressed, yes, but he also looked a little scared.

"You're a bit better with that gun than I feel comfortable with," he half-joked.

"What can I say? I'm American. They don't give you your passport unless you can kill balloons with BBs."

"Got it. Maybe there's something less scary I can try," he said, scanning the stalls for games that didn't involve guns. His eyes landed on a booth where you kicked soccer balls into a makeshift goal. "That one," he said, striding over to it.

He got in several good kicks, winning me a prize. I chose a squirt gun from among the selection. Maybe I do have a thing with guns.

After all the shooting and kicking and witty repartee, we took a break in the refreshment tent. Over two cool beers, we talked about places we'd like to visit.

"I've been to Germany several times but it never gets old. I'd like to go back to Berlin," Mika said.

"Me too! I visited a friend there a few summers ago but only for a few days. I'd love to see more of it."

"OK, then. Let's go."

Was he serious? I mean, obviously he didn't mean right now but, like, he wanted to go on a trip with me? Cool.

"And I've always wanted to go to Iceland. To swim in the Blue Lagoon and stalk Björk, even though I'm sure she's not there often."

Mika laughed. "Count me in! Well, not for stalking but for the rest of Iceland, sure."

Now we've planned two trips together? Either he's going to turn into a gushy French romantic and scare me off, or I just might end up marrying this guy.

"Deal. But no shots in our beer or I'll puke," I said.

"Huh?"

I told him the story of the Beer Cocktail Extravaganza.

"Don't worry," he said, unable to hide the horrified look on his face. "We'll stick to regular beer."

Maybe I shouldn't scare off my date so quickly by shooting guns and telling stories about vomit, but, hey, the sooner he knows the real me, the better.

As we drained the rest of our beers, I wondered what we should do next. We'd already planned enough trips, that's for sure. "Wanna ride the Ferris Wheel?"

"I'd love to," he said, grabbing my hand.

A short wait later, we were on top of the Ferris Wheel. What a view! We had a direct shot of the modern pyramid in the courtyard of the Louvre. How romantic.

On paper the date probably seems cheesy, but as I was living it, I enjoyed every minute of it. I was in Paris, with a gorgeous guy, a gorgeous view, and a slight beer buzz.

I couldn't wait to see where this ride took me.

19

Björk and Bacon

"Everything's better with bacon." Mika's new mantra was music to my ears. We'd fallen into a routine of going out a few times a week and cooking dinner at my apartment the remaining nights. The menu *chez moi* ranged from *haricots verts* wrapped in bacon (delicious) to mac and cheese with leeks and bacon (super delicious). We even tried chocolate-bacon cupcakes (not so delicious).

I enjoyed being with a French guy who could adapt to the American style without losing his French identity. You don't want a pushover but you don't want a bossy, know-it-all either. He was definitely a keeper, this one.

Had I lucked out at last?

Six weeks into our relationship we took the trip to Berlin we'd talked about on our first date. We made silly poses in front of statues and ate insane amounts of food. We got fake stamps on our passports at Checkpoint Charlie and took a somber look at remnants of the Berlin Wall.

"You know, I met Gorbachev when I was eleven years old," I said to Mika.

"What? No way!" he said, clearly impressed.

"Yep. Shortly after the fall of the Berlin Wall, he came to none other than Fulton, Missouri to give a speech about the end of the Cold War. It's the same site where Churchill gave his famous Iron Curtain speech back in the 40's, at Westminster College. My mom and step-dad let me skip school to watch. The stage was decorated with huge slabs of the Berlin Wall. It was hard to hear because the interpreter's voice echoed but it was a moving speech. The next day at school I did a presentation."

"So how did you meet Gorby?"

"After his speech, he walked to his limo, surrounded by bodyguards. But then all of a sudden he turned and walked toward the crowd and shook hands with a few people. I was one of them. I remember him smiling at me. Pretty cool."

"I'll say! Any other former heads of states you've met? Any Communist friends I should know about?"

"Nah, I think that's it."

We glanced back at the Berlin Wall, lost in a rare moment of silence.

"So... where to next? More historical sites?" Mika suggested, looking as if that was the last thing he wanted to do.

"Not really. I'd honestly prefer a beer right now."

"Ha, that's exactly why I like you," he said, wrapping his arm around my shoulders. "I'm glad you don't want to spend the whole time in stuffy museums."

"And I'm glad I don't have to pretend I want to just to impress you. Now let's drink some of that famous German beer."

❧

A few weeks later, I casually reminded Mika that my birthday was approaching. I didn't want to pressure him, especially so early in our relationship, but I didn't want *nothing*. Taking me out to dinner would have been perfect.

"What are you whispering about?" I asked one night at the Swedish Society after returning from the restroom. Mika and Anne Marie had guilty looks on their faces.

"Nothing you need to worry about," answered Ammo, giving Mika a conspiratorial wink. What were they up to?

The next day, Mika announced he had picked up a part-time job. Proud to be dating a Frenchman with a strong work ethic (I mean, he already worked full time at a four-star hotel), I didn't think much more of it. I just figured he could use more cash. Who couldn't?

On the night of my birthday, Mika had a funny smile on his face as he handed me a card. *A card?* I stopped myself. A card was fine. I didn't need him to spend money to show he cared.

I slowly opened the envelope, savoring Mika's reaction. Given his anticipation, there had to be more than a card in here. *Please don't be a love poem. I might gag.* I stopped myself again. Could I be any more ungrateful? Just open the darn thing and get on with it!

"Oh my God. You're taking me to *Iceland?*"

"Yeah," he said with a sheepish grin. "I mean, if you want to go."

"Ha, aren't you funny. You know I want to go! I've been dying to go. And you promised on our first date that we would go!" I was amazed. So *that's* why he'd gotten a part-time job. Wow. I almost felt like I couldn't accept it. "This is the best gift I've ever gotten!" I shouted.

How did I end up with such an awesome guy?

Back from our Nordic getaway, and fresh-faced after a

natural-minerals scrub in the Blue Lagoon, we were a full-on couple. We hung out nearly every day and hadn't gotten sick of each other yet. I noticed we were spending more and more nights in, eating and watching TV. In fact, our relationship included lots of eating. Maybe we could add a few strolls around town to our repertoire before my clothes got too tight.

"You're turning into a right old married couple, you's are," Anne Marie said one evening when the three of us were out on the town. "I hardly see you anymore."

"We're here right now, so quit your bitchin'!" I said.

But it made me wonder, was she right? Mika and I had been spending a lot of time together and a lot of time at home. To me it seemed like the perfect amount but was it too much? Or maybe too much too fast?

"Oh, Ammo. You're just jealous because you want a piece of me," Mika tried to say with a straight face before we burst out laughing at the absurdity of it. Mika couldn't pull off arrogance if he tried. And while he was a few years younger than me, he was nearly ten years younger than Anne Marie. Cute as he was, I don't think she wanted "a piece of him."

We clinked glasses. "Cheers to the lovely couple," Anne Marie toasted. "I hear them wedding bells already."

20

Something to Prove

Strolling the streets of the City of Light, it was apparent the holiday season was upon us. The French don't shy away from Christmas decorations the way many overly politically correct American establishments do. The town is covered in light displays and greenery and nativity scenes, all with a certain Parisian chic to them.

As charming as it was, I bid *adieu* for a few weeks to visit both sets of parents in the US.

"I'm looking forward to heading home for the holidays," I said to Anne Marie over a pint of cider. "But I can't imagine being away from Mika for two whole weeks."

"What, are you two's joined at the hip, you are?" she teased in her Irish accent. "It'll do you good to get away from each other for a while before you turn into a couple of old married farts."

I gulped down my drink, afraid she might be right. Would I become lame now that I had a serious boyfriend?

Or would I keep my Party Girl identity, the one who danced on tabletops and passed out on bathroom floors? Or would this be the perfect chance to find some balance in my life, perhaps keeping the tabletop-dancing but nixing the bathroom-floor-sleeping?

The night before my trip, we all went out partying. It started out innocently enough, but the events that followed changed my partying policy forever—I no longer allow myself to drink the night before an international flight.

I simply can't be trusted.

But that night I didn't know or didn't care. I wanted to prove that, yeah, OK, maybe I was spending a lot of time with my new beau but I could still party with the best of them. I was young and cool, not old and married.

I went a tad overboard with my point-proving. If by "tad" I mean "so far overboard even a lifeboat couldn't save me."

Let's not share exactly how much I drank or else my mom might check me into rehab, but let's just say it rhymes with Schmoo Bottles of Schmampagne and Schmour Shots.

"Hey babe, I don't mean to be a drag, but shouldn't we be getting home?" Mika dared to ask. "It's nearly 4:00 and you have to be up in a few hours."

I shot him a look that could kill. "What? Who cares! Let's live for tonight and worry about tomorrow tomorrow. Now where are those shots?"

Make that Schmoo Bottles of Schmampagne and Schmive Shots.

თ~ℒ

The next morning (or three hours later, take your pick), I heard a knock on my door. *Go away, I don't want any.*

More persistent knocking. "What?" I wondered aloud, lugging myself out of bed. "Ohhhhhhhh, fudge. That must be Mika."

I answered the door to my boyfriend's shocked expression. "Um, we need to go but do you maybe want to take a shower first?"

Glancing in the mirror, I saw what he meant. I looked as bad as I felt, which was horrible. "Yeah, I'll just be a minute."

Fifteen minutes later, I was somehow showered and dressed, though I'm pretty sure I missed a few spots. It's hard to reach everywhere when you're leaning against the shower wall.

Faking like I felt better than I did, so as not to let him know he had been right the night before, I grabbed my purse. "OK, I'm ready to go. Do you want me to drive?"

He had borrowed his parents' car to take me to the airport and I thought that by driving, I might feel less queasy.

"Um…." he stalled.

"What?" I asked, flinging my arm out to make a point. However, in doing so my purse knocked over a chair, landing on the floor in a loud thud. Whoops. Maybe the alcohol hadn't completely worn off yet.

"No offense but maybe you're not totally sober? I don't mind driving."

Man, this guy was good. How had he not said "I told you so" yet? I would have been rubbing that in his face if the roles were reversed. Though they never would be—he would never be so irresponsible.

"Good idea. You drive. Let's go, then?"

"After you," he said, picking up my suitcase.

It took me forever to walk down the five awful flights of stairs. This was going to be a long ride. I had to say it. "You were right, you know. We should have gone home when you said so. Probably even sooner."

He let out a smile before quickly covering it up. "Well, we all have our nights like that."

He never had nights like that but I didn't want to make myself look any worse. He had let me off the hook without rubbing it in, which was way more than I deserved.

❧

As bad as I felt, it paled in comparison to what happened once I boarded the plane. Warning: graphic vomit scenes up ahead. If you can't handle it, I suggest you skip a few pages or visualize puppies running through a field.

Before passing security, I bought a sandwich (salami and pickle, which I would regret in the very near future) and we sat on the floor while I tried to eat it. The airport was spinning. How would I endure a 10-hour flight? Thinking about it made my stomach turn.

"Sorry I'm so hungover," I said to Mika. "But now we don't have to worry about a drawn-out tearful goodbye. I can't even hold my head up for longer than two seconds."

"Are you going to be OK?" he asked, his concern showing clearly on his face.

"Do I have a choice?"

"Good point. Well, try not to think about it," he said, rubbing my back. "I'm going to miss you while you're gone, but at least I'll finally get to bed at a reasonable hour." He looked at me with an amused smile, one I was growing quite accustomed to by now.

"Ha, ha. You'll miss me more than you can imagine, Lesage, just wait and see."

❧

After finishing the last bite of my poor choice of a sandwich, I headed to security. Mika and I said a final goodbye, then continued to wave to each other the entire time I waited in line. Sweet, but it was making me dizzy.

A too-short-while later, I was buckled in my seat and not feeling any better. Ready for the longest, most painful flight of my life. Knowing the hangover was all my fault didn't help.

"You will find your flight information card in the seat back pocket in front of you," the flight attendant announced, rattling off a slew of other safety instructions.

Speaking of the seat back pocket in front of me, I should look for a barf bag. The salami and pickle sandwich (seriously? What had I been thinking?) threatened to make an appearance and I needed to be prepared.

I rummaged through the pocket, finding the in-flight magazine, SkyMall, and the safety card, but no barf bag. Another victim of airline cutbacks. Well, maybe I wouldn't need it.

My stomach churned as we taxied for what seemed like hours. *Are we driving there or flying? Get a move on!* I tried not to think about how sick I felt, but it was pretty much the only thing on my mind. Puppies running in fields transformed into puking puppies running in fields. Ice cream sundaes turned into puke-cream sundaes.

OK, let's think. We could only taxi for so long before the beast eventually had to take flight. From that point I only had to wait until the fasten seat belt sign was turned off and then I could rush to the toilet. Ew. Throwing up in an airplane restroom? What a terrifying thought.

If I only knew how the day would end, I would have been begging for the chance to throw up in an airplane restroom.

I counted the rows to the lavatory. Eight. Could have been better but could have been worse. *I just have to make it ten more minutes, then run five seconds, and I'm safe. I can spend as much time as I need once I'm locked in the stall, I just need to make it there.*

The guy in the seat next to me darted surreptitious glances my way. I guess I did look suspicious, rifling through the seat back pocket and scoping out the plane. Did he think I had some sinister plan to take down the aircraft? Or could he simply tell from the green hue of my skin that something horrific was brewing?

I smiled weakly and tried to keep the vomit at bay. *2,3,5,7, 11… uh oh.* My nifty trick to count prime numbers couldn't stop the inevitable. The vomit was making its way up and there was no stopping it.

To this day, I wonder why I didn't get up and run to the restroom. True, it's a violation of airplane security but surely that would have been better than what happened next.

By now you're thinking, "So what? She pukes on a plane. I saw this coming a mile away." Did you, Smarty Pants? Well, let's just say the first draft of this story was way more gruesome. But due to some loving editors who care about your sensibilities, we've decided to end the story here. If you want details, imagine the worst scenario possible and multiply it by 10, and then you'll get what I *wish* happened. Multiply it by 10 more and you'll be close to what did happen.

Let's fast forward, shall we?

ৼৼ

The rest of the flight passed slowly, giving me plenty of time to regret my decisions from the night before. What had I been trying to prove? That I could party like I used to? I never used to do *this*. This was way over the top. Sure, it had been fun in the moment, but was definitely not worth the resulting pukefest-slash-hangover.

And I hadn't even gotten to say a proper goodbye to Mika! Half-heartedly waving while trying not to throw up was not the romantic way I'd hoped to part before the holidays.

That's it, I decided. *Just because I have a boyfriend doesn't mean I'm lame. Why had I thought it would?* I could still party, but I didn't have to party "like the good ol' days." Mika and I could go out sometimes, stay home sometimes. What mattered was that we were happy together. And we were. I had nothing to prove.

"Here you go, honey," the flight attendant said as she handed me a ginger ales and a packet of pretzels. Accepting them gratefully, I realized all I had to prove was that I could make it the rest of the flight without vomiting on anyone. After that, it might be time to settle down a bit.

Or at least drink fewer than two bottles of champagne and five shots in one night.

Confessions as My Relationship Gets Serious

Wrapping Christmas presents, the radio tuned to the All-Christmas, All-the-Time station, my mind wandered. I missed Mika, but at least I had the comforts of mac and cheese and Taco Bell.

After setting the presents under the tree and returning the wrapping supplies to Mom's designated gift-wrapping bin (wonder where I get it from?), I whipped out my journal.

Though Mika and I had agreed to boycott the local boulangerie after the mean lady behind the counter had been an insufferable cow one time too many, I snuck down there for a sandwich when I was really hungover. It was either that or McDonald's, and the insufferable cow had the sole redeeming quality of being closer.

Ammo and I always criticized married people, saying that they turned lame once they tied the knot and never went out anymore. And it only got worse with kids. We swore we would never let that happen to us. But... that was before I met Mika. Now it sounded kind of nice. I mean, of course I still wanted to party-that side of me would be hard to shake permanently-but I found myself wanting to do it less and less.

Was I growing old or just growing up?

21

Taking the (Mini) Plunge

Spending the holidays with family was a welcome blast of love and comfort food. I stuffed my face at holiday party after holiday party, passing on the eggnog of course, and blathered on about my new beau to anyone who would listen.

"It's been a great trip, sweetie," Mom said as she dropped me off at the airport at the end of the visit. "I'm gonna miss you."

"I'm gonna miss you too, Mom. I'll call you when I land."

"Thanks, you know I appreciate knowing you're safe. Now hop out before the security guy comes over." Every airport drop-off with her was the same—even though there was a special area for dropping people off, which would allow you to linger over your goodbyes, my mom always went to the pick-up place.

"What? I've been doing it this way for years. I don't see

any reason to change," she would say if I tried to suggest a different plan.

I hustled out of the car, grabbing my suitcase and shouting "I love you, Mom" as she hauled ass out of there, nearly swiping the security guy.

As I waited in the check-in line, I lit up at the thought of seeing Mika. Would he be as happy to see me as I was to see him? Or had he enjoyed a quiet two weeks without me? Or both?

The minute I saw his expectant face as I exited customs, I had my answer.

"Those were the longest two weeks of my life," he said.

"Me too! Next time, you're coming with me." I wrapped my arms around his waist. "I missed you so much!"

"Same here," he said, giving me a kiss. "Now let's get home and eat. Unless you wanted to stop for a drink first?" He winked.

"Ha, ha. No I won't be having any drinks, thank you very much. I've learned my lesson."

I hadn't truly learned my lesson—there were a few more wild nights in me (stay tuned!)—but the Airplane Incident had definitely knocked me down a few notches. I no longer felt the need to party like a crazy maniac. Maybe just a regular maniac.

ço~ço

A few weeks later, I received a letter informing me that my landlord was selling my apartment. I had the option to buy it or move out. It was surprisingly affordable for a Parisian apartment but I wasn't interested in buying such a small place. If I was going to buy, it would need to be a smidge bigger. But that tiny bit bigger would take it well out of my price range.

So for now, I'd stick with renting. Which meant

moving. Again.

"Where do you think I should move?" I asked Mika over a homemade dinner of mac and cheese with bacon one night. Mika lived in the 12th *arrondissement* with his parents, while I'd always lived in the 15th. "I could move closer to you but I'd prefer somewhere around here."

"Oh, don't move closer to me. I was hoping to move out soon anyway. Actually..." he paused. "Do you want to move in together?"

My heart fluttered. Not much could get me to stop eating mid-mac and cheese but this definitely qualified.

"Really? It does make a lot of sense. But I'm more of a neat freak than you realize. Are you sure you're ready?"

"I'm 100% positive. I've been thinking about it ever since you left for Christmas."

Awww. He was so sweet. And clueless. He had no idea what he was getting into. Even I could admit that I was difficult to live with. My touch of OCD combined with the small size of Parisian apartments, well, let's just say this would put our relationship to the test.

"OK, let's do it!"

৩৶৶

We scanned apartment listings in the area, but always found a fault. Too expensive, super ugly with 70's-style mustard-colored tile, a bathroom in the hallway (not the hallway of the apartment, the hallway of the *building*. This is more common than you'd think.)

Eventually, we found one that met our criteria and made an appointment to visit. It had been completely redone—the walls were sparkling white, the kitchen had a fridge, the bathroom was in the apartment. Our standards weren't super high, so this apartment met all of them.

"We'll take it!"

"Do you have your dossier?" the real estate agent

asked, with a tone that implied she was sure we didn't have a dossier.

"Do you have a stick up your butt?" I wanted to ask. With her tight black suit, fashionably tied scarf, and perfectly coiffed hair, she thought she was God's gift to real estate. As my dad would say, "She thinks she's hot snot on a golden platter but she's really cold boogers on a paper plate." Good thing Dad and I never went apartment-hunting together or I'd never get a new place.

I covered my distaste with a smile, knowing I needed to stay on her good side.

"Oui, bien sûr," Mika said, handing her a stack of papers that included his paystubs, my rent receipts, bank statements for the both of us, and a few DNA samples. What else could she need?

"D'accord, but doesn't she have pay stubs?" Hot Snot asked, pointing at me. "And what about a guarantor to ensure you pay your rent? Can your parents do it? Also, don't you have any rent receipts, monsieur? And you two are not married?"

Her flurry of questions wiped the smiles right off our faces. We'd already supplied so much, yet she wanted more? Let's break this down:

Paystubs for me.
If I didn't work in this country, I couldn't have paystubs in this country. I explained this but she didn't seem to understand the concept of working remotely or being paid in another currency. I guess they didn't cover that at Hot Snot Real Estate School. I offered to provide my American paystubs but she said that was no good.

Guarantor.
I understood the reasoning behind this but I was adamantly opposed to it. In France it's hard to evict people from their apartments, even when they're degenerate losers

who are years behind on their rent. And if you do anything as abhorrent as, say, shut off their water in an attempt to shoo them out, you'll be labeled a slumlord.

As a result, landlords take it out on good people like us and make our mommies and daddies sign a paper agreeing to pay our rent if we become degenerate losers. From the owners' perspective, I understand they're protecting their investment. From my perspective, I feel like a child.

Which matched my sense of humor but still.

Did I really need my parents to cover me? And even so, my parents weren't worthy of this honor since they didn't live in France. So that meant we needed Mika's parents to do it. That was a big favor to ask when he and I had been dating for less than a year.

Rent receipts for Mika.

Apparently Hot Snot never read the book *Catch-22*. How could Mika have rent receipts if no one would rent him an apartment? Someone had to be the first to take a chance on him!

Get married.

Now wait just a minute, lady. We're already taking a big step moving in together and now you want us to get married? Again, I understand the perspective of the landlord—a married couple is less likely to split up than a boyfriend and girlfriend. And if we split up, the person who remains is less likely to be able to cover the full rent. But from our perspective, what are we supposed to do? Even if we rushed to get married, this apartment would be rented out by the time we had all the paperwork.

ক্ষত

Needless to say, we were discouraged. Having lived at home up to this point, Mika had never suffered through this. And I had lucked out for one reason or another with my previous apartments. But now we were in the big leagues. We were looking at apartments in a higher price range, so the landlords were understandably more concerned about getting their monthly fee.

What were we going to do?

❧

After studious searching, Mika discovered an agency that catered specifically to expats living in Paris. An agency that didn't give a hoot which country your paystubs came from, as long as you had money. We did have a little of that.

We scanned their website listings and found one in a classic stone building in the 15th *arrondissement*. "That façade looks familiar," I said, clicking for more photos. "No way—it's *my* building!"

Not only was it in my building, it was on the 5th floor too! I wasn't thrilled about trudging up those stairs but if we got this apartment, at least moving would be a breeze. Just scoot everything down the hall and be done with it.

Or so we thought.

The good news: we'd been accepted, thanks to our impressive 40-page dossier. The bad news: the apartment was located on the 5th floor of the *other* building, the one across the courtyard. Which meant we had to move everything down five flights of stairs, then up five flights of stairs, then walk down five flights of stairs and back up five flights of stairs for the next load.

Maybe it wouldn't be too bad. How much stuff could a twenty square meter apartment hold anyway?

Answer: a lot. It didn't look like a lot because I was über-organized (that'd be the OCD), but it added up. Plus, while I'd previously only had my clothes, laptop, and fan to drag to this apartment, I now had several pieces of furniture to my name.

Sigh. Of all the places I could have moved in Paris, I moved as close as possible while still encountering as much difficulty as possible.

We began with gusto, biting the bullet and moving items one by one methodically down and then up the stairs. On the twentieth trip, I dropped a potted plant, breaking the ceramic vase, and thanked God I only had to carry it down to the trash instead of up the stairs of the next building.

After ten more painful trips, we were sweaty but done. I flopped down on my new couch, legs still shaking from exertion.

Home sweet home!

ॐ॰ॐ

Next I had to prepare for the walk-through at my old apartment.

Technically it had been rented as "furnished." Many Parisian landlords do this, not to make it easier on you, but because they're allowed to have one-year leases on furnished apartments, whereas leases on unfurnished apartments run for three years. So while the landlords have to supply the furniture, at least they can kick you out after a year if you're a deadbeat. Sounds like a good deal. You get furniture, they get peace of mind. Paradoxically, it often lowers the rental price since the landlords aren't as worried about not receiving their monthly rent check.

And it is a pretty good deal. In theory.

In practice, you often get crappy furniture that even scavengers would reject. In fact, most of the time these urban treasure hunters *have* rejected it.

How do I know?

When I moved in to my old place, it was lovingly furnished with an ugly table and three hideous chairs, all of which had a tell-tale layer of grime that could have only come from one place—sitting on the sidewalk.

Walking around Paris, you'll find random pieces of furniture stashed in front of aromatic bakeries and bustling newsstands. People clean out their houses and set the remnants on the sidewalk for someone else to take. Technically you're supposed to call a special trash service and they'll pick it up for free but the few times I've done that, the item was gone before the trash collectors came.

One time, I set an obviously broken lamp on the curb on my way out for the evening and before I rounded the street corner, it was already gone. In less than two minutes, my trash had become someone else's treasure.

You can get fined if you set an object on the curb without having called the pick-up service (when you call they give you an ID number that you're supposed to write on a piece of paper and tape to the object), but I doubt that law has ever been enforced since even broken pieces of junk get picked up before the trash crew arrives. I don't mean this as a slam to the garbage removal service—they normally arrive within a few hours. I just doubt an object has ever lasted that long on the streets of Paris.

Except, of course, for the table and chairs that had occupied my former kitchen. If people who take broken lamps didn't even want this crap, that gives you an indication of how horrible it was. No way would I keep that filthy furniture in my apartment, but I would lose my deposit if the apartment wasn't furnished when I did the final walkthrough.

Sniffing the air, I had detected the distinctive odor of urine. Deposit be damned, this furniture had to go. I lugged all four pieces down all five flights, with a superhuman ability to block out the horrid smell. Dusting my hands off, I looked in both directions. A tall, thin man approached from the left and a mother with two kids strolled toward me from the right. With potential takers on the horizon, I left them to do their business in peace.

Sure enough, when I checked a few hours later, my furniture was nowhere in sight. What on earth do people do with this stuff?

Fast-forward to the final walkthrough at my old apartment. With my own furniture out and the original furniture long gone, I now had to "refurnish" the apartment. Shouldn't be too hard.

Mika and I took to the streets. "How about you go left, I go right, and we meet back here in thirty minutes?" I proposed.

A half hour later, he had a table and I had two grimy, mismatched chairs. Almost there! As he carried the loot upstairs for cleaning, I scoured the neighborhood again. One more chair was all I needed. It didn't matter how dirty or how ugly.

Come on, come on! Worst case, I could have bought a new chair but I was sure I could find one. *Just one more street...* Sure enough, I found a plastic lawn chair (what was that doing in the middle of Paris?) leaning against a trash bin.

I raced home and showed it off to Mika. "Not bad, huh? I'll take it from here," I said, scrubbing the last of the chairs while he tried to cool off. Bummer that we already moved the fan to the new apartment.

After a final wipe-down, I set my fancy new furniture in the middle of the room. This would have to do. The walkthrough was the next morning, and I had made it in the nick of time.

৩৯০৫

"Bonjour," I said, letting the landlord into the apartment the next morning.

"Bonjour," he replied, pulling a dossier out of his bag. "Let's do this quickly and you'll be on your way!"

I stood still as he examined the place. Scattered nail

holes decorated the walls but other than that it was pristine. My furniture stood absolutely still, too, hoping to pass for the original furniture he'd stocked the place with.

"One table, check. Three chairs, check," he said, with merely a passing glance before heading to the bedroom. He dashed through the rest of the tour and reported I'd be getting my full deposit back.

Whew.

❧

Back in our new apartment, despite the boxes cluttering the place, it already felt like home. I wrapped my arm around Mika's waist as I surveyed all the work to be done.

"One good thing about living with me is that I can whip this into shape by the time you're done fixing dinner," I said with a smile.

"I know," he said, grinning. "We make a great team."

22

Dust Off the Résumé

"Man, those stairs never get easier!" I tossed my keys on the table and collapsed onto the couch. Gloomy winter had turned to a slightly-less-gloomy spring, and Mika and I were comfortably settled in our new place. He kept the toilet seat down and I kept my nitpicking to a minimum. We were getting along quite well in the modest space.

However, my work prospects were risky. Freelancing sounds great—taking vacation whenever you want, charging high hourly rates, and, in my case, stuffing my face with croissants while in the comfort of my jammies. The less glamorous side (you mean less glamorous than croissant flakes on my shirt?) was not having a steady paycheck.

I'd secured several retainers, which ensured a certain amount of monthly income. I delivered quality work on time and aimed to exceed client expectations so they would engage me for future projects.

But as the years wore on, my clients transitioned to local resources instead of "the girl who works in her apartment in Paris." Despite my reasonable rates and assured availability (if not sobriety) at all hours, it was understandably less convenient to work with me than someone closer to their offices.

With a deep sigh, I decided to look for a job in France.

I'd held out for so long but now here I was, thinking of joining the workforce I'd made fun of for years. Would I become lazy or was that just a stereotype? Would I go on strike every other day? Would I leisurely get my coffee and give *la bise* before starting work, or would I keep my American habits?

There was only one way to find out.

Sitting in my comfortable home office, I opened my web browser and entered the URL for—you guessed it— Craigslist. One posting practically screamed my name. A mid-size French company wanted an American to handle their US marketing. My skills and experience matched perfectly. And not to brag, but I could speak English pretty well.

I polished up my CV (that's résumé, for all my compatriots), described in a cover letter why I was so incredibly perfect for this job, crossed my fingers, and clicked "Send."

I looked down at my jammies with a wistful glance. If I got this job, I'd have to wear real clothes. And wake up at a reasonable hour. I'd been spoiled by the time difference for all these years; I could roll out of bed at 11:00, go to the gym, eat lunch, start work at 1:00 and still be ahead of my East Coast colleagues.

Was I ready to wake up early and hustle alongside other city folk on the always-hot Métro?

I tried to picture this new life. Despite the comfort of my yoga pants (not that I did yoga, I just liked the pants), it could be a nice change. Clicking down the sidewalk in my heels, reading a book on the Métro during my commute, and leading important meetings in French.

Of course, I had to get the job first. And a work visa. Oh dear God, a work visa. As if it hadn't been hard enough getting a blasted tourist visa, now I was going to change my visa status.

Maybe I should rethink this...

ॐॐ

A few days later I received a call to set up an interview. At least I think that's what the fast-talking French speaker said. She gave me a time and an address, which I hoped I'd copied down correctly, and wished me a good day.

Woo hoo! I'd gotten a callback! So either I was awesome or they were desperate. I'd soon find out. Assuming I could find the place.

The next morning I showered and dressed and was putting the finishing touches on my makeup when Mika woke up. "Wow, you're up already? That's a first!"

"I know! It's crazy. I'm not even tired. I'm pumped! Let's go!"

"OK, calm down. I still need to take a shower," he said, climbing out of bed. "Is there any coffee left?" he asked hopefully.

"Sorry, I downed it all. Why do you think I'm so hyper? I overcompensated, I guess. Don't worry, I'll make another pot for you." Man, I was jittery. I needed to chill if I was going to impress them in my interview.

Twenty minutes later, we were out the door. We rode the Métro together to Concorde, before switching to take line 1 in separate directions. How cool! If I got the job we could do that every day!

We stood on opposite platforms waiting for our trains, me waving to Mika like a big, huge dork. I really needed to get out more. My train arrived a minute later and carried me all the way out to La Défense, the business district of Paris. Technically it's not even in the city of Paris, it's so far out.

Nearly everyone on the Métro at that time of day is on their way to work, so everyone was dressed nicely and reading newspapers. I blended right in with my sharp black dress, stockings, and heels.

I found the office with a few minutes to spare. Whew. The next obstacle would be the interview. Well, that and making sure I hadn't replied to some scammy ad on Craigslist where they were actually serial killers luring people into their lair.

A smiling receptionist greeted me as I walked in. OK, so, probably not serial killers. "Vous pouvez attendre ici et Gabriella va venir vous chercher." I waited in the lobby for the person interviewing me to arrive.

Moments later, a gorgeous South American girl greeted me and I followed her to a conference room. "Vous préférez parler en français ou en anglais?" she asked me.

"I can speak French but I'm much funnier in English," I joked. Idiot! This wasn't a comedy routine. Why did I say that?

Fortunately, she laughed. "OK, no problem. We'll do the interview in English. Let's get started."

Gabriella could see I was a good match for the job. Now that the coffee had worn off, I was able to articulate my experience and goals. Working from home in my pajamas for the past five years made me fear I'd lost my touch, particularly in face-to-face situations. But I resumed my former professional air and came across as a competent candidate.

"Those are all the questions I have," Gabriella said. "Let me find my boss so he can talk to you."

Already made it to the next round! I sat in the silent conference room and imagined working there. The open plan office was fun and funky, with young, trendy employees. Not how I'd pictured a French office, but then again, what did I expect? People smoking and wearing berets and saying "Non, non, non!" all the time?

"Hello, I'm Laurent," a tall, thin guy with reddish hair and hipster glasses said as he entered the room. His French accent gave him away, but I was thrilled he was speaking English. "So you're from the US?" he asked.

If this was the type of interview question he threw my way, this would be a piece of cake. "Yes, from St. Louis. It's in..."

"Yes, I know it," he jumped in. "It's in Missouri. I lived there for a few weeks on an exchange program. Great town."

He had to be kidding. Not only had he heard of St. Louis (and knew it wasn't in *Louisiane*) but he had actually lived there?

"I agree. Great town. Of course, not quite as nice as Paris, which is why I moved here," I said, transitioning the conversation.

We moved on to more typical interview questions, and judging by his reaction, I'd done pretty well. All that was left was for them to hire me!

"Thanks for coming in. We'll be in touch."

I crossed my fingers tightly. This could be it!

Weeks passed and I heard nothing. Bummer. I had foolishly thought it would work out. I should have realized it would be too easy to get the first (and only) job I applied to, but it had seemed like such a great fit.

I reluctantly checked back on Craigslist and other job sites but nothing looked right. That really had been the only job for me, a sparkling oasis in the middle of depressing jobs I was either overqualified or underqualified for.

On the bright side, at least I could stay in my jammies for a while longer. And spend more time with Mika.

We rotated between the Swedish Society, the Long

Hop, and relaxing at home. We took weekend trips here and there, touring the Scottish Highlands and the Loire River Valley.

One weekend we hopped the border to Belgium with his parents.

I'd met Catherine and Gilbert a few months prior for a leisurely lunch at their house. I'd been apprehensive but Mika assured me it wouldn't be fancy.

They opened the door, greeting me with two kisses on each cheek.

"Bienvenue! Please, come sit down," Catherine said, nudging me over to the dining table, where they proceeded to stuff me with five courses of French delicacies, topped off with wine and champagne. All of this in the midst of their homey apartment with the TV on in the background, their living room lined with Gilbert's teddy bear collection from around the world. A multi-course meal in a French person's home had the potential to be a snobby, stuffy affair but instead I felt relaxed.

The wine helped.

As I got to know his family, I could see Mika had gotten his dark hair and friendly smile from Catherine, and his height and laid-back attitude from Gilbert.

Mika and I quickly fell in the habit of lunching at his parents' house every other Sunday. They welcomed this American girl with open arms, even if they didn't always understand my accented French.

As we headed out on a bright Saturday for our first road trip together, I wasn't sure what to expect. Would we get along as easily as we did over wine-filled lunches?

Gilbert backed the compact Chevrolet out of the parking garage and we all crammed in. En route to Bouillon, Belgium!

The picturesque town was right across the France-Belgium border, a three-hour scenic drive through the French countryside. Even with the air conditioning blasting in the front, the cool air didn't quite make it to the back. Good thing I'd loaded up on deodorant.

Once outside the Paris city limits, Gilbert stopped at a gas station to fill up the tank, gas being much cheaper out there. "Pick any snacks you want and we'll meet you at the check-out," he said.

We were kids in a candy shop, loading up on donuts and junk food (yes, they do have that in France). When we met Catherine and Gilbert at the cash register, we noticed their selection was nearly identical to ours. I fit right in!

We enjoyed our treats over espresso, then hit the road. I was predictably car sick the entire time but it was still an enjoyable ride. We pulled over to take photos in front of a huge boar statue, as I marveled that France had random roadside attractions like in the US. Maybe they didn't have the world's largest ball of twine, but this was just as impressive.

The sun was high overhead when we arrived in Bouillon. We wandered the cobbled streets, choosing a shaded restaurant along the river for lunch.

"Order whatever you like," Catherine said. "It's our treat."

"And order lots of beer. Belgian beer is the best," Gilbert added.

Free beer? Twist my arm! But remembering we still had a three-hour car ride home, I restrained myself to just two of the high-alcohol-content brews. See? I *eventually* learn my lessons.

Energized from the meal, we climbed a hill to the town's famous castle.

"Amazing, don't you think?" Gilbert asked.

"It's beautiful." The immense fort offered a breathtaking view of the town in the valley below, and I nearly wore out my camera batteries taking it all in.

"And now for the most important part of the trip," Gilbert said, as he motioned for us to follow him back down the hill.

The "important" last stop was a grocery store to stock up on Belgian beer. While available in France, the potent brews were way cheaper this side of the border. We wheeled the shopping cart to the cash register, beer bottles rattling conspicuously as the locals eyed up the alcoholic French family. I would have been ashamed if I hadn't gotten such a great deal.

Trunk and bellies full, we headed back to Paris, me drooling on Catherine's shoulder as I dozed in the backseat.

Mika's parents acted as my parents-away-from-home. Gilbert had the same sense of humor as my dad (juvenile, sometimes offensive, always hilarious) while Catherine's favorite pastime was the same as my mom's—talking. I considered myself lucky to be part of such a welcoming family. Particularly one that appreciated food and beer as much as I did.

23

Goodbye, Twenties

Before I knew it, my 30th birthday crept around the corner. Yikes. Thirty?

I was in a pretty good place—awesome relationship, decent apartment, pretty cool work-at-home gig. But I couldn't help comparing myself to my friends back home. Many of them were married, owned houses, and had bigshot jobs. Not that it was a competition, and clearly taking a few years out to live in Paris had affected my timeline, but I wondered if I was moving too slowly.

"So what do you want for your birthday?" Mika asked.

"Nothing, really. After last year's trip to Iceland, I'm set for life!" Though I could think of one thing I wanted. "But, um, like, maybe not for my birthday but maybe sometime kind of soon I would want, um, a ring?"

"A ring? What kind of ring?"

"You know, a *ring*," I said, looking into his eyes.

"Ah, I see. A *ring*. Well, your birthday is a bit soon, but what about Christmas? Or New Year's?"

Wow. Was this really happening? Talking about marriage? You mean I could actually broach the subject with my boyfriend, as opposed to waiting three years and then ransacking a suitcase behind his back? Mika's willingness to discuss it was refreshing.

"Surprise me," I said. "I don't want to rob a Frenchman of his chance to be romantic. But I'm happy we're on the same page."

ço~ç

Headed home for the holidays, this year I was sober as could be. Lesson officially learned. No more throwing up on planes. And now I was able to say a sufficiently sappy goodbye to my future fiancé before dying a slow death in the endless security line.

"I'm going to miss you," I said, hugging him around the waist.

"It's only for a week. Then I'll be there, too," Mika replied, kissing the top of my head. "Time will fly, don't worry. And as soon as you get to Taco Bell, you'll probably forget all about me."

He had a point. I could almost taste the Double Decker Taco Supreme as he spoke. "I'll call you when I land," I said, giving him a kiss.

"You better," he said with a smile, as we finally broke away from each other.

We could be stars in the world's cheesiest chick flick if we went on any longer.

ço~ç

A week later, my stomach was in a flurry. Mom and I had baked a ton of Christmas cookies that morning and I'd eaten way more raw dough than I should have.

"It's all the sugar," I said to her.

"Are you sure it's not because a certain someone is arriving today?" she asked. It was December 26th, so if Mika stuck to his word (and I had every reason to believe he would), I would be engaged within the next five days. No wonder I was hyped up.

"How am I going to make it until 5:00? That's ages from now!" I whined. I may have been thirty years old but that didn't stop me from acting like a kid around my mom.

"Well, definitely don't eat any more cookies or you'll be even more wound up," she said.

৩৽৵

At last 5:00 arrived and I borrowed Mom's car to pick up my beau at the airport. The 20-minute drive felt like an eternity. The overhead monitors said he'd arrive in the C concourse, so I waited outside the security exit by the C gates. The next 30 minutes were agony.

I paced back and forth.

I hopped from foot to foot.

I counted floor tiles. I counted ceiling tiles.

I had just started reciting prime numbers when I saw a tall head bobbing out of the corner of my eye.

He was here!

We stared at each other, goofy smiles on our faces as he closed the distance. Once he was out of the concourse, he scooped me up in a huge bear hug.

"That was the longest week of my life!" I said.

"I know! I missed you too. But I'm here now," he said, giving me a smoochy kiss.

Noticing some prudish onlookers, I cut the smooch-fest short. "Enough mushy stuff. Let's get your bags." We walked hand-in-hand to baggage claim.

I was super excited to see Mika but an itty bitty part of me was let down that he hadn't proposed to me yet. *Chill, woman*, I thought. *Let the man breathe the St. Louis air before you jump on his case!* I'd assumed the ring would be burning a hole in his pocket during the flight and that he'd want to unload it as soon as possible. And since we'd be surrounded by family the rest of the trip, I'd thought he'd want to get it over with at the airport. That's not very romantic, though. *Again, woman, chill. He'll do it when he's ready.*

"Luggage from flight 2314 will be arriving on carousel 4," an announcement blared.

"That's my flight," Mika said, as he steered me to a sign with a large number four marked on it. He scanned the room in every direction. I glanced around to see what he was looking at. Why was he being so weird? When I turned back to him, he was holding a ring.

Ohmygod. It's happening!

"It may not be romantic, but my hands are sweaty from gripping this thing so tightly ever since I left Paris. I'm afraid it's going to fly out of my hands if I wait any longer. And anyway, since our first date, we've always talked about travel and then we actually went on all the trips we said we would. So airports are kind of our thing. And it shows that when we say we'll do something, we do it. I'd love to travel with you the rest of my life. I'm rambling. I'm kind of nervous. Anyway, will you marry me?"

Could he be any more adorable? "Yes!" I shouted. "Of course I will! Now let me help you out by taking that ring off your hands."

He handed over the entire ring box, hands shaking. I wanted to slip on the ring but first I gave him a huge hug, and then a not-so-short kiss. Puritan bystanders be damned, I just got engaged! I'm entitled to a public display of affection.

I felt him calm down in my arms. "Don't worry, now it's my ring to lose. You can relax," I said with a smile, sliding the ring on my finger.

"Do you like it? I picked it out by myself. I wasn't sure if it was your style."

"It's perfect," I assured him. Though I was so in love I probably would have found beauty in a Froot Loop. "I hope your bags come out soon. I can't wait to tell everyone the news!"

అఎౖ

I tried not to stare at my brand-new ring as I drove us to the Christmas party for Doug's side of the family.

"I'm gonna give my dad a quick call," I said to Mika. Because talking on the phone while driving is way safer than admiring a ring.

"Cool, I'll call my parents at the same time."

It was the middle of the night when Catherine and Gilbert picked up the phone, but they were thrilled with the news. "*Félicitations!*" they called down the line.

At the same time, my dad offered his congratulations. "And good luck to Mika, he's really in for it." Hey! What's that supposed to mean?

The party was more of the same. "Congratulations, but watch out, she's a live one!"

OK, I know I can be feisty and Mika is famously calm, but he knows what he's getting into. And if he doesn't, then shhhh, don't tell him!

24

Work Papers

The distinct ringtone of my cell phone pierced the air, knocking me out of my dreamy engagement reverie. I'd been doing a lot of that lately. But why not? You're only engaged for a relatively short time so might as well enjoy it while it lasts.

Engaged. To a tall, dark, handsome Frenchman. I'd be disappointed about being a walking cliché if I weren't so damn happy!

When I answered the phone, it was the speed-talker from the company I'd interviewed with a few months prior. I'd nearly forgotten about them amidst all the wedding excitement!

"Hello, Vicki? Yes, something super fast, you're hired. Something else super fast, something that doesn't even sound French, work papers, start in a month?"

"Oui, pas de problème," I said, hoping I'd grasped the most important parts of the conversation.

I was hired! My life had really changed. One minute I was a single party girl and now I was a nearly-married working professional.

Now for this pesky work visa. Though I was engaged, I wasn't going to speed up my wedding for work papers. And even that wouldn't be quick. Like it or not, I would have to endure the visa renewal process again, this time with a whole new set of paperwork.

At least I had Mika to help.

❧

A few weeks later, Mika accompanied me to my appointment at the *Préfecture*. We arrived at 8:30 for the 8:50 appointment. Factoring in the long wait while the employees gave *la bise* and caught up on gossip, I figured we'd be right on time.

What I hadn't counted on, though, was having to wait outside before even being admitted to the building. The mile-long line (that's like 32 kilometers) moved ever so slowly since only ten people were allowed entry at a time. As you had to pass a security vestibule (understandably so—these government workers were so infuriating I could envision a disgruntled civilian coming in for payback), they could only process that many people at once.

But the most annoying part was that at 8:30 they hadn't even opened the doors. Great. Once again I was early to an appointment but would likely be late through no fault of my own.

At least there was some decent entertainment—a group of protesters gathered in the plaza facing the *Préfecture*. They wore panda masks, though I couldn't ascertain why. Perhaps as a sign of peace? I heard that pandas are actually mean. Or maybe that was their point? "We seem peaceful but we'll rough you up if we don't get what we want! Grr!" Who knows.

From their garbled shouts, I made out something about immigration. I wasn't sure if they thought France allowed too much immigration or not enough immigration or if they simply thought the line to enter the immigration building was too long.

In addition to their fear-inducing masks, some group members wore signs decorated with a letter. They stood in a line so that the signs spelled a word:

R E G U A R I S A T I O N

French not being my first language, I figured it was a word I didn't know. "What's 'reguarisation'?" I asked Mika.

"I have absolutely no idea," he said, his face scrunched up as he tried to work it out.

The moment of revelation came when I spotted "L" taking a smoke break. I'm not one to judge (except that I totally am), but isn't it a bit early to be smoking? And not just early in the morning but early in the protest? I mean, what time did they arrive? The *Préfecture* doesn't open until 8:30 (or more precisely, 8:37) so I can't imagine it's worth their time to protest much earlier than that. So why's "L" already taking a break?

She stubbed out her cigarette and rejoined the group, sliding in between "U" and "A."

"Régularisation?" Even with the additional letter I still didn't get it. "Do you know what that means?" I asked Mika.

"Um, yeah, something about conforming to a law. I'm not sure how to say it in English. Do you say 'regularization'?"

I didn't know. Did we? It was way too early to be straining my brain like this. Why couldn't they use a more common word for their signs? And perhaps if they chose a shorter word, people could take smoke breaks without confusing bystanders. And perhaps if the stupid *Préfecture* would open the doors I wouldn't have to overanalyze stupid signs!

Eventually they let us in, thankfully before my visa expired. After waiting to check in and then waiting for my number to be called, I was finally perched on a seat in front of Sandrine the Mean Government Worker. But this time I was armed with my French fiancé to assist with any questions.

Funny thing, though, when a company is willing to pay the fee for a working visa (which is much higher than the fee for a tourist visa), all of a sudden the paperwork goes through without a hitch. So after one *rendez-vous*, I was approved.

Sandrine almost seemed disappointed things had gone so smoothly. She released me from the bureaucratic walls with a temporary card (though "card" is a loose term—it was almost as big as a sheet of paper) that would allow me to start work immediately.

I was officially a French employee. Coffee machine, here I come!

25

French Kissing at Work

The big day was here. No, not my wedding. At least not yet. My first day of work. In France. Was I ready for this?

It might not have been such a big deal if I'd done it straightaway. But after years of listening to complaints about the French system from expats and Frenchies alike, I was apprehensive.

Oh well. It was a bit late now to change my mind. I didn't suffer through mounds of paperwork to chicken out at the last second and stay home in my jammies.

I hung my pajamas on their hook. So long, old friends. I'll see you tonight, if I survive.

Entering the lobby of my new office, the same friendly receptionist greeted me. However, I learned that Gabriella no longer worked there. Ack! I'd been counting on at least one English-speaking colleague to ease the transition.

Fortunately the receptionist promptly introduced me to

Marie, who was as welcoming as she was fluent in English.

"Hello! Happy to have you here. Let me show you around and then later we can do lunch. Sound good?"

Back on track. She showed me to my desk, pointing out the coffee machine on the way. Of course. "Laurent will meet with you when he arrives. Until then, I guess you can just do whatever it is you were hired to do!"

That wasn't much to go on, but it was enough. I'd had months to brainstorm ideas and I was raring to go.

As I sat at my desk, drafting a marketing plan, the other employees trickled in. Each one came to my desk, introduced themselves, and gave *la bise*. Friendly lot!

However, over the course of the next half hour it became a tad annoying. Not to be a grump but how could I concentrate if I was interrupted every minute? No sooner had I started to type my next idea than another colleague would show up and greet me with cheek kisses.

I decided to just go with it (as if I had a choice), hoping it was just a first-day ritual. But the next day was the same! One by one everyone filed by my desk, giving *la bise*, asking how my first day went. I appreciated their niceties, but how would I ever finish my marketing plan?

I realized it wasn't just a newbie thing—everyone greeted everyone individually. *Bises* flew everywhere. Taking a quick headcount, I tallied nearly 50 employees. If each person gave each other person *la bise*, then using the Gauss method of counting[14], that would mean 1,225 shared

---

[14] And you thought me counting prime numbers was dorky! You had to know by now that I would do the calculation. In case you're curious, the Gauss method is actually quite simple: You take the total number of people kissing (in his theory, it's handshakes which is probably just as germy but less French), subtract one, then multiply by half. This is because you don't kiss yourself (unless you want people to think you're weird) and then you pair everyone off after that since me giving you *la bise* is the same as you giving me *la bise* (it only counts once). In the case of my productive work environment, that's 49x25, or 1,225. Technically *la bise* is comprised of two kisses, one on each cheek, so

kisses. I don't even want to know how many shared germs.

After the fatiguing Tour de Kissing, everyone needed coffee. This easily occupied another 30 minutes waiting in line at the coffee machine. Then they would saunter back to their desks, boot up their computers, and start the day.

At this point it was nearly time for lunch, so if you needed to meet with anyone, you had to grab them before their tummy rumbled and they lost focus.

French lunches can last anywhere from thirty minutes (rarely) to over two hours. They're supposed to last one hour but no one ever seems to be in a hurry. So you have to wait until around 2:30 for everyone to file back in from lunch. But hold on! No one can resume working before the post-lunch coffee.

Past 3:00 you can safely ask a coworker for help or organize a meeting, but you'd better wrap it up by 5:00 so they have time to shut down their computer before leaving.

༄༅

If it were up to me, I would have skipped *la bise* altogether and shouted a generic "Hello" in the open space. But as I tended to arrive before everyone else (I can't help it, I like to be early), I had no choice but to let them file past for *la bise*, day after day.

It was bad enough being interrupted non-stop, but then you would get the occasional commenter.

"Oh, what a long email you're writing!"

"Wow, that spreadsheet has a lot of numbers."

"What are you working on?"

I wanted to respond saying "It's a project called Nunya Bizness" but as I was still new, I should be polite. It's a harmless question, but how am I going to get any work done if I have to explain what I'm doing to everyone who

that's 2,450 reasons nothing ever gets done in France.

walks by? And why do they even give a hoot?

Eventually I learned the perfect balance. I avoided working on anything too exciting, too colorful, or with too many words or numbers, lest it attract their eagle-eyed interest. But I had to work on something, not only to maintain a good work ethic, but to show the *bise*-giver that I was too busy for a chat.

I settled on checking my email, responding only to the messages that wouldn't require too much text, or reading brief industry-related news articles. Shame I couldn't dive into the task of my choosing, but it was the only way to keep the kissing fools at bay.

26

Bureaucratic Welcome to France:
Part Un

Now that I was a full-fledged member of the French work force, the government wanted me to partake in two orientation sessions. Given that I could do both during work hours, I had no problem with that. I could use a break from all the kissing.

First up was an afternoon at the OFII (Office Français de l'Immigration et de l'Intégration—it's as exciting as it sounds), a crumbling concrete block of a building near the Bastille.

"Bonjour, je m'appelle Yvette. Welcome to France! I will be guiding you through your orientation this afternoon," she said in French with a bigger smile than the situation warranted. But who knows, maybe this would be the best orientation of my life?

"Today you will complete various tasks. At the end of

each task, you will receive a certificate. Hold on to this document for dear life because it is the only proof that you have completed your orientation. Copies are not acceptable. Do not lose them or you will have to retake the class."

Got it. I certainly didn't want to endure this snoozefest again.

"Now," she resumed with that out-of-place smile, "it's time for the film!"

We were treated to a movie about living in France, with the theme that women are equal to men, have the right to vote, and can't be forced to marry. No less than three times they reminded us that beating our wives is not permitted by law in this country. Noted!

The highlight of the video, which was entirely in French, was when they stressed the importance of learning the French language. Our quality of life would improve! Finding a job would be much easier! The beret would sit on our head much more comfortably! Agreed, but if we understood what the video said, we probably already knew French.

"Did you all enjoy the video?" Yvette asked.

"I thought it was great," a guy in the back said, with no hint of sarcasm. Dude, keep quiet so we can speed this along!

"Wonderful!" she exclaimed. "Now remember, once you receive your certificates, hold on to them carefully. You don't want to lose them!"

Oh, I *don't* want to lose them? Glad she cleared that up.

"Now I'd like to explain the program for the rest of the afternoon. Please save your questions for the end."

A hand shot up in the back.

"Sir, I see your hand but as I just said, I'll answer all questions after I'm finished," she chirped. "OK, after this, you will stand in the hallway and wait your turn to be called. An interviewer will assess your level of French to determine if you need French classes, and if so, at which level you should start."

Questions rang out throughout the room. "Which hallway? Which door? When will she call us? What if my French isn't good enough?"

"Great questions everyone! I will answer each and every one when I'm done with the entire program," she said. How was she able to stay so polite?

"Some of you will receive a certificate straight away, if your level of French is adequate." I rolled my eyes, knowing what was coming next. "Keep this certificate in a safe place because if you lose it, it cannot be replaced." She paused for emphasis. "The interviewer will also assess if you need to attend the 'Living in France' class, where you learn how to go to the bank and the post office and call emergency numbers. We also offer a class on how to find a job in France."

"What number do I call in an emergency?"

"Do you have a listing of available jobs?"

"Everyone, please. I will answer all questions at the end. Now, where was I? Oh yes. Next you will wait in a different hallway and will be called one by one for your medical visit."

"Which hallway?"

"Your medical visit," she continued, "will consist of an eye exam, a chest x-ray, and several other quick, non-intrusive examinations."

"What kind of examinations?"

"How intrusive?"

"No questions, please. After your examination, you will receive a certificate. Please keep this certificate in a safe place. Don't lose it because it cannot be replaced. You will then return to the waiting room-"

"The same waiting room?"

"You will return to the same waiting room and wait until your name is called, then you will receive your chest x-ray in an envelope. Keep this x-ray in a safe place." She paused to make sure we understood that in addition to finding a safe place for our documents, we'd now have to find a safe place for our x-rays. I don't know if she thought we lived in a flood zone or a cardboard box. How unsafe did she think our houses were?

"What temperature do the x-rays need to be stored at to keep them safe?"

"Before we leave this room, I will issue you a certificate," she continued, blatantly ignoring the man's question. "It will certify that you've watched the video and completed part one of your orientation. I will call you up one by one and sign your certificate. Please keep this certificate in a safe place, because it cannot be replaced."

I was beginning to think this part of the class could have been conducted by video as well. Or even a sheet of paper with the schedule on it and a note, copied five times, telling us to keep our certificates in a heavily guarded safe.

We get it! Move on!

"So, how many certificates is that in total?" the man in the back asked.

"Five certificates plus the chest x-ray," the teacher replied, before realizing she had accidentally answered a question before the end. The man looked triumphant. She looked heartbroken. "But no more questions!"

She stared around the room, daring us to ask another question.

"Lastly," she said, the smile returning to her face, "I have some great news for you. While you wait for your name to be called, you can enjoy the lovely refreshments on the back table."

Thirty chairs squeaked as we turned to see the arrangement so lovingly set out for us. Water, apple juice, and some janky cookies. Good thing I'd eaten already.

"OK, now, does anyone have any questions?"

Crickets. Now that the group knew there were snacks,

no one wanted to waste a precious second with questions.

"None? OK then, bon appétit!"

The group descended on the snack table like a flock of vultures. (Technically a "venue of vultures," if you want to be a know-it-all.) By the time I made my way over, all that remained were overturned cups and cookie crumbs, scattered about like shrapnel from a cheap food bomb. It's like these people had never seen food before. What would they have done if there hadn't been any snacks—eaten their folders?

A glass of water would have been nice, but I'd have to survive without one. I returned to my seat and waited for my name to be called. I couldn't wait to get my hands on this amazing certificate we'd heard so much about. Then I'd only have four more, plus a chest x-ray, to go before I could blow this joint.

The only other person who hadn't gone for the snacks presumably hadn't done so because he was knuckle deep in his nose-picking adventure. When God invented folders, He didn't think this guy would be wiping so many boogers on them. Gag me. I hoped that folder wasn't the "safe place" he was planning to keep his certificates.

In a group of thirty people, I was 28th to be called. Sigh. But considering we had a long line of tasks ahead of us, it didn't matter much. Video-watching certificate in hand, I progressed down the hall to wait for my French interview.

A gruff, heavyset woman opened the door and shouted my name, retreating into her office before I had even made it halfway to the door. A few awkward, long strides later and I was in.

"Bonjour," I said with a smile.

"Bonjour," she barked.

Yikes. I was nervous that I wouldn't pass and would have to take a 20-hour French class, or maybe even two, depending on which level she assessed me. And worse, my classmates would likely be the same weirdoes from today.

My French was passable in most situations, abhorrent in the crucial ones, and fluent after a few drinks.

Damn, I should have had a drink first. I needed to pass or else my next few nights and weekends would be spent with this sorry lot.

Reviewing my file she said, "Vous résidez en France depuis cinq ans déjà, c'est ça?" You've been living in France for the past five years, right?

"Oui," I replied.

"Et maintenant vous commencez à travailler pour une enterprise française?" And now you're working for a French company?

"Oui," I replied again. I wasn't sure if she was looking for a longer response but my one-word answers seemed to be doing the trick so far.

"Ah, bah, vous parlez très bien le français, non?" Ah, so, you speak French very well then?

"Je parle le français, mais je ne suis pas sûre que je le parle bien." I speak French but I'm not sure if it's very well.

She chuckled. Imagine that, I got Ms. McGruff to laugh! "Don't worry, you speak very well. Here is your *certificat*," she said, as she signed it with a flourish.

Some test! I'd said less than 20 words and she'd given me a passing grade. Though you did have to be decent at French to understand her rapid-fire questions and respond correctly.

She scribbled her signature on the certificate for the "Living in France" course, assuming I'd learned how to use the bank and post office after half a decade of living here. And since I already had a job, she signed the "How to find a job" certificate, handing it to me with a satisfied expression. I wasn't the only one happy for the speedy exchange!

I tucked my certificates into the safety of my folder (you don't have to tell me twice! Or six times!) as I scooted back my chair. "Merci, et bonne journée!"

Next up: *visite médicale*. Let's see what the teacher meant by "non-intrusive." The eye exam was a cinch, I just had to read letters off a chart. I always have a hard time pronouncing letters with a French accent—"G" sounds like "J" and vice versa—but fortunately neither appeared on the chart.

The doctor took my weight, and either I'd eaten too many croissants or their scale was off by a few kilos. I said as much to her and she winked as she handed me my certificate, then told me to remove my shirt for the chest x-ray.

As an American, this was the worst part. Europeans parade around topless beaches like it's nothing but for me, walking topless into the x-ray room was super uncomfortable.

I tiptoed in, embarrassed beyond belief. And this is coming from someone who has slept on a bathroom floor. Fortunately, the x-ray techs were so engrossed in gossip they hardly noticed me.

Last but not least, after yet another waiting room spell, an elderly doctor called me in to his office to review my results. He said my x-rays were "beautiful" (a superlative my mom would likely use) and sent me on my way. "Remember to hold on to that x-ray. You never know when you might need it!"

I bounced out the door, free at last. Well, weighed down by five certificates and an x-ray, but free nonetheless.

27

Bureaucratic Welcome to France:
Part Deux

Almost done with my Integration in France, all that remained was a day-long orientation session about French history, culture, laws, and other stuff. It didn't sound half-bad.

The next week, I arrived for the class at 8:50. We'd been warned that anyone arriving after 9:00 would be denied entry and would have to take the class another day. No way would I cart myself to the far end of the 18th *arrondissement* only to be refused the privilege of taking this class!

The massive wooden doors opened precisely at 9:00, and a pleasant government worker showed us to our classroom. Over the course of the next 30 minutes, she took roll. The class consisted of no more than 20 students so I'm not sure how it took 30 minutes to call roll.

At 9:25, two students snuck in. Hey! Not fair! But the teacher was so lost in check marks and hard-to-pronounce names that she didn't notice.

Once roll was painfully called, our perky teacher provided an overview of the program. "We will learn about French history and culture. It's going to be exciting!"

I'll be the judge of that.

"Then we will break for lunch. Or should I say, a FREE lunch." A few eyebrows raised around the room. "That's right! Your lunch is paid for by the French government. Free lunch! Then we'll learn more about France and its laws. If we finish early, then you're free to go! Oh, and I will issue you a certificate at the end. Take care not to lose this certificate, because it cannot be replaced. The only way to obtain another certificate is to take the class again."

"But at least we would get another free lunch!" an enthusiastic Brazilian guy said.

She laughed as if it was the most hilarious thing she'd ever heard, which, considering she worked here, was entirely possible. "True! OK, are we ready to get started?"

It was nearly 10:00. We'd been ready for the past hour! But I had to admit the learning bit could be fun. I knew a lot about France already from school and from having lived here for five years, but I could always learn more. The lunch I was not as optimistic about, mainly because the teacher had hyped it up too much. She had to be covering something up.

What had me most concerned was this Brazilian character. I'd been through enough bureaucratic hoops to know his type—the jokester who uses these classes as his comedic platform. That would be bad enough, except the teacher had dangled the possibility of leaving early in front of us and this wannabe stand-up was going to blow our chances.

"We'll begin when France was settled by the Gauls."

Oh wow, we were really going back. No wonder this class took all day.

As she progressed through France's history, aided by a text-heavy power point presentation that didn't match up to what she was saying, I listened in a drowsy relaxed state. With no test at the end, I didn't need to take notes or stress if I missed a piece of information. That didn't stop the Brazilian guy from scribbling furiously in his notebook and raising his hand every few minutes.

"...France's pride and joy is Monsieur Renault, who manufactured the first automobile." Hold on, what? I think I missed something. Did she say that Renault made the first car? Did she mean the first car in France or the first car, period? Because I'm pretty sure that was a Mr. Henry Ford, with his famous Model T. I scanned the power point slide but found no mention of a car, only a space shuttle and a high-speed train. Was France rewriting history here? Or were we Americans mistaken? Or had I simply misunderstood?

"The first car manufactured in Brazil was a Chevrolet," our friend from the southern hemisphere informed us. Thanks for sharing, buddy.

Perky Teacher moved on to some other tidbit and I stopped worrying about it. Who cared who created the first car? Just keep moving.

"Well that's all I have planned for this morning. Now, who's ready for lunch?"

We filed out of the building, Mr. Brazil enthusiastically leading the way. We passed several nice restaurants, falsely getting my hopes up. Our final destination turned out to be your average restaurant, not too horrible but nothing worth harping on about all morning.

I took a gander through the menu and settled on *steak-frites*, a Parisian classic. How could you go wrong with steak and fries?

A harried waitress came over. "Your lunch has already

been started and will be out shortly. The menus are for paying customers only."

Well, excuuuuuuuuse us! We weren't skipping out on the check. Our food was being paid for, just not by us. And she hadn't even given us the option of ordering off the menu and paying for it ourselves so she didn't need to be so snotty about it.

My classmates and I waited in uncomfortable silence for the food to arrive. One girl at my table tried in vain to strike up a conversation.

"Vous venez d'où?" Where do you come from?

"Les Etats-Unis. Et vous?" The US. And you?

"Le Cameroun." Cameroon.

Silence. No one else at the table even bothered to speak up.

The kitchen door burst open and with it came the strong aroma of fish. It smelled rank, and only got worse as she set the plates down in front of us. Two beady eyes stared at me. Head, tail, scales and all. I didn't even know where to start. A modest portion of rice off to the side was the only redeeming quality of the lunch.

"You are being served this delicious fish so as to accommodate all religious inclinations," Perky Teacher informed us before deboning the fish with the ease of a cartoon character. I swear, she stuck the whole thing in her mouth and just pulled out the skeleton.

But she and Mr. Brazil were the only ones actually eating it. As I checked everyone else's plates, no one had touched the fish. If no one was going to eat it, seems like we could have gone for *steak-frites*.

I suffered through the bony fish, knowing the afternoon would seem that much longer on an empty stomach. After saturating the rice in salt (you're welcome, blood pressure) I made a decent meal of it.

Then, the *pièce de résistance*: dessert. The waitress burst through the kitchen door again, looking at our hopeful faces with an expression that said, "You saw the fish. I wouldn't get too excited about dessert," then set 6-packs of plain yogurt on the table.

The heck? I was pissed off on so many levels. First, she couldn't even separate the 6-packs? Maybe she knew she'd be back in 5 minutes to pick up the untouched containers to serve them to tomorrow's crowd, so she was saving herself some trouble.

Second, *plain* yogurt? I hardly want to eat yogurt for dessert anyway but at least throw a little fruit in there to fancy it up. Plain is just cruel.

But lastly, and most importantly, I'm 100% against yogurt as dessert. Dessert is supposed to be fun! Fattening! Indulgent! It's not supposed to offer probiotic benefits for only half the calories. Screw you and my health! I want calories!

కావ

The yogurt for dessert phenomenon is quite common in France. Which I find weird, partly because it's just weird and partly because this country is known for wonderful pastries like *éclairs* and *macarons*. How can a nation that produces such decadent treats be content with bland yogurt?

I eat yogurt, don't get me wrong. But I eat it for breakfast. Not as the grand finale to a meal.

There's this French commercial where everyone shows up for a dinner party and this one chick brings a 12-pack of yogurt. All the people at the dinner party are like, "Yay, thanks! Now the fun can begin!"

Mika showed me a parody of the commercial and it's hilarious. Same set up, with a dinner party and a chick bringing yogurt, but this time the host says, "Qui a ramené cette merde?" Who brought this shit? Then they chase the girl and someone draws a knife.

I feel their pain.

I'd be pissed if I went through the trouble to cook a lovely dinner and my guests brought nice wine and baguettes, and then some dummy shows up with yogurt for dessert. That's like giving out toothpaste on Halloween. Thanks, but you suck.

I wasn't in quite the same righteous position during my free lunch, so I kept my thoughts to myself. But no way was I eating room temperature plain yogurt and calling it dessert.

Perky Teacher scooped up a container with a flourish and said we were free to roam the *quartier* as long as we were back to the classroom by 2:30. Faster than you could say "Ciao, suckers," we stampeded out of there, some people already lighting cigarettes, others dialing their phones. I killed time reading a book while relaxing on a nearby bench.

"Ready for class?" a voice shouted from behind me. My new Brazilian friend.

"Ready as I'll ever be," I groaned. I was stuck with this guy for the five-minute walk back to class.

"What was your favorite part about class this morning?"

Was he serious? "It's hard to pick one part. It was all great," I said. Might as well have a little fun.

"I see your point. It really is interesting, huh?"

This guy was incredible. He was truly having a good time. In a way, it was better to be like him. He loved life and everything it threw his way, even French orientation classes. To each his own, but he better not drag the class out any more than necessary.

"Did everyone have a nice lunch?" Perky Teacher asked as we filed to our seats.

"It was wonderful," the Brazilian guy responded. No one else said a word.

"Our next topic is taxes," she started, before being interrupted by a loud bang.

We turned in the direction of the noise and saw a guy that almost literally had birds flying around his head. Though none of us had seen the action, it was apparent he had walked into the glass door head on. What's funny is this was one of the dirtiest glass doors I'd ever seen. There was even a sign taped to it. How did he run into it?

He shook his head, reoriented himself, then opened the door. He nonchalantly entered the classroom and sat down, as if nothing had happened.

"And who are you, sir?" the teacher asked.

"I'm Jean-Paul Dupont. I'm here for the class."

What? No. No, no, no. This guy couldn't waltz up here at 2:30 and think that was going to fly. Clearly the rest of the class agreed, and the girl from Cameroon said, "Nuh-uh. If he didn't have to eat that fish, he doesn't deserve a certificate."

"Yeah!" we shouted in agreement.

The teacher calmed us down. "Shhh, class. Don't worry. Sir, you needed to arrive by 9:00. You are welcome to stay and learn about taxes in France, but you will have to come back another day if you'd like to receive your certificate."

The guy was an idiot but he wasn't that dumb. He scurried out of the room, mumbling about coming back later. We all watched, hoping he'd run into the glass door on his way out, disappointed when he made it through safely.

"OK, it's tax time!" Perky Teacher could hardly contain her excitement.

The conversation was surprisingly interesting. First, she explained that every French household with a TV has to pay an annual TV tax. I'd never known this since I guess

Pierre paid it in our old apartment and I hadn't had a TV since then (I love you, Internet). At first, I was appalled to have to pay tax each year just for owning a TV. But then she explained that the tax pays for the public channels. French TV doesn't have nearly the amount of commercials as American TV, so maybe it's worth paying extra at the beginning of the year to be done with it?

Our Brazilian amigo didn't agree. "That's scandalous! What if I only watch DVDs? I still have to pay for the public channels?" He looked around, trying to bring us into the discussion. I saw his point, but I was more concerned with leaving on time. I wasn't missing happy hour for this guy.

The teacher then brought up another interesting tax-related topic (who knew there could be more than one?) Some guy had been working under the table since 1987 and discovered a month prior that since he hadn't received any paystubs and had only been paid in cash, he was not eligible for social security. Which makes sense since he never paid into the system and there's no proof of him working in France. But she told the story as if we should feel sorry for the guy. Um, no. Why would I feel sorry for someone who a) is so damn dumb that he didn't realize in 20+ years that he was clearly being paid under the table and b) hasn't been paying taxes for 20+ years? There's your retirement fund, buddy. Check your pockets!

I glanced over at Mr. Brazil to see which side of the debate he was on, but even he had gotten tired of his enthusiasm. He just stared at the teacher, waiting for her to set us free.

After listening to La Marseillaise (the national anthem), which gives me chills with pride for my adopted country every time I hear it, we finally received our certificates.

"Now remember..."

"Keep it in a safe place!" we shouted in unison. If we learned one thing from this class, it was to guard the certificate with our lives.

I checked the time. 4:55. Could have been better, if Captain Brazil kept his trap shut, but could have been worse. I basked in the sunlight as I walked to the Métro. I was now officially, at least according to my *certificat*, integrated into France.

A fishy burp escaped my mouth before I could stop it. Ick.

This better be worth it.

28

The Calendar Year

Certificates and x-ray safely stowed at home, I was ready to hit the ground running at my new job. Except it was mid-June. For me, June meant warmer temperatures and chilled wine. For the rest of France, it meant closing up shop for the summer.

By law, salaried employees receive five weeks of vacation, but it's not uncommon to receive nine or even eleven weeks, particularly for those who've been with the same company for a long time or work for large French mainstays. Small businesses can shut their doors for three weeks straight, leaving only a hastily scrawled note taped to the door indicating their return date. *Boulangeries* thoughtfully provide a list of other bakeries in the neighborhood, lest you be stranded baguette-less in the street.

Offices remain open, but with a meager workforce. Even if people don't take their entire five weeks in the summer (opting for a more modest month-long stretch), you'll find that at any given time, only about half the staff is present.

This, among other uniquely French customs, affects the entire work year.

Let me break it down for you.

In January, everyone wishes their friends, family, acquaintances, neighbors, butchers, bakers, and candlestick-makers a happy new year.

"I wish you health, happiness, and good fortune for the entire year, and best of luck with all your personal and professional endeavors."

It's a freaking mouthful.

You have until the end of January to share your good wishes for the year, so it's not uncommon to be stopped by a colleague on January 28th and have to stand there for five minutes while they politely run through their spiel.

You've gotta credit the French, though, for their impeccable memory. They always remember who they've exchanged greetings with and who they still need to wish well. That's a lot to remember over the course of thirty-one days.

Combine new-year-wishing with the morning ritual of *la bise* and you've used up all of January just being polite.

February is when the real work starts, maybe because they know they only have 28 days of it.

The French give it all they've got (for the requisite 35 hours per week, that is) until May, which is jam-packed with holidays. May 1st is Labor Day and one week later is World War II Remembrance Day, which commemorates the end of the war in Europe. Falling on different dates, but often in May, are the religious yet nationally observed holidays of Ascension and Pentecost Monday.

If a holiday falls on a Tuesday or Thursday, the French will usually *faire le pont* ("make the bridge") and take off the corresponding Monday or Friday to make a long weekend.

Depending on how the days fall, you could have nearly half the month off.

In June, knowing everything's coming to a halt soon, employees are averse to beginning any new projects. But they will diligently wrap up existing projects (of which there are many, since no one did jackshit in May).

Any attempts at progress during July and August are futile. It's a good time to dust off your shelves, clean out your inbox, and drink an extra cup of coffee or two.

September is one of the best months to be in France. Fresh energy abounds as everyone is relaxed from vacation. They'll kick off projects, make decisions, and get the ball rolling. Invigorating!

They keep this momentum through the end of November, but as soon as the first Christmas decorations go up, their productivity goes down. For the rest of the year, it's party-planning-this and holiday-shopping-that.

Adding it up, you've got about six good months of work. Half a year.

Incredible.

ৎৎ

Now as fans blew papers off desks in the open office, I could see the vacation mindset had already set in. Fortunately, Laurent gave me an assignment with a member of my team who'd already taken his vacation. We completely redesigned our Facebook application and were ready to launch at the end of the summer. I couldn't wait for my colleagues to review it when they returned from vacation.

"Never ask a French person their opinion," Mika warned me.

"Why not? It will be good to have everyone's feedback, especially since I'm still new and don't know everything about the business yet."

"If you ask ten people their opinion, you'll get eleven different responses," he said, with no hint of irony in his voice. "Seriously, be prepared."

What did he know? Other than being French.

My situation was different. I had drafted a simple yet thorough test plan in an Excel spreadsheet. All my colleagues had to do was go on Facebook (which, let's be honest, half of them were probably already logged into), play with the app, then fill out the corresponding sections of my spreadsheet.

Foolproof, right?

I re-read and edited my email, closing with "Any feedback is appreciated—thanks for your help!"

I clicked send and held my breath, hoping the tests would go well. Sure, people would have suggestions and they would probably find a few bugs. That was to be expected. But hopefully they would be impressed with the app overall and provide useful feedback on the aspects that needed to be changed.

Wrong. Of course I should have listened to Mika.

My inbox pinged as I received responses from my colleagues.

"Your email has a typo in it."

"Your Excel file is in .xslx format. It should be converted to .xls."

"The columns in your spreadsheet are too narrow."

"We normally use a different font for our documents."

"I don't have any comments other than the ones everybody else already provided."

They were missing the bigger picture. Did any of them even test the app? I wasn't asking for feedback on my spreadsheet, I was asking them to *use* the spreadsheet to provide their feedback! Why were they making this so difficult?

As I sat at my desk, modifying my spreadsheet to be 100% crystal clear, another email pinged in my inbox. What now?

App looks good so far, but found two errors on home page. Can you check them out?

- Laurent

Someone who had provided feedback on the app itself! Although it would have been infinitely more helpful if he had specified the errors.

I walked over to his desk to ask for clarification. But he wasn't there. Weird. I knew he was at the office because he had come by to do *la bise* that morning.

I clicked back to my inbox and read his email, then noticed the telltale "Sent from my iPhone" signature at the bottom. *Uh-oh. I know what happened.*

Sure enough, two seconds later Laurent emerged from the restroom, looking down at his phone instead of where he was walking. Ew! He sent me that email from the bathroom! Someone finally tests my app and they have to multi-task?

I couldn't leave the email in my inbox—it had been in the bathroom! Scrolling past it would give me cooties. I wrote myself a note to remember to test the home page, then filed his message away so it couldn't contaminate my inbox any longer.

 educ

Mika couldn't have been more right about French people having a comment for everything. While their feedback on my spreadsheet had been annoying, at least it was on-topic. What grated on my nerves even more were non-work-related comments. Case in point: my water glass.

We've heard repeatedly that we should drink eight 8-ounce glasses of water per day (about two liters) to enjoy all sorts of health benefits. I religiously drank more than that, figuring it would balance out all the wine. Our sparse office kitchen provided tiny cups, slightly bigger than shot glasses, that were not only inefficient water receptacles but were always dirty.

To avoid spending all day washing dishes and fetching water, I brought a Guinness pint glass from home. I only had to fill it four times throughout the day, providing a reasonable number of breaks while still being productive. Such a simple thing should go unnoticed, right?

"Wow, that's a big glass!"

"Are you drinking beer at work?"

"You must love beer!"

"Is Guinness your favorite beer?"

"I don't like Guinness."

"You sure drink a lot of water!"

"How many of those are you going to drink today?"

"How long does it take to fill a glass that big?"

"You must really like water."

Had these people never seen water or a large glass before? Why did they have such a burning desire to know about my cup?

"Did you get that glass in Ireland?" the sales manager, Theo, asked one day after I'd topped it up.

I was half-ready to smack the guy until I realized it was a decent question. A normal conversation-starter coming from someone who wasn't bizarrely curious about a glass, just wanting a friendly chat.

"Yep, it's from the Guinness brewery tour. Have you been to Dublin?" I asked.

OK, so this question passed, but what about the other 90%? What's a girl gotta do to drink in peace?

29

Teacher's Pet

As the months wore on, I became more accustomed to my work environment. I filled my water glass before people arrived, providing one less opportunity for interrogation.

A side benefit of working with French people was that my French improved exponentially, which Mika's mom complimented me on every time I saw her. I'd given a presentation to 45 people, and even though it was riddled with grammatical errors, I delivered it without dying of embarrassment. Knowing champagne was waiting for me helped.

Confidence is key when you're learning a language. Many French people know English way better than they give themselves credit for, but because they're not absolutely perfect, they often keep their talent secret.

I didn't have that luxury. I had to speak French in most aspects of my job so I was forced to improve.

One day, Marie and I met with a potential business

partner. Meeting with my familiar colleagues was one thing, but a salesperson from the outside? I had to be extra professional and do my best to positively reflect the company's image.

"Si je comprends bien, vous avez une application pour les mobiles qui a la même cible que nous?" Marie asked.

"Oui, tout à fait," the salesperson responded.

"D'accord, nous vous écoutons," Marie said.

I nodded throughout the conversation, understanding every word. Pretty cool. I understand everything they're saying. Look at me, in my French meeting with French people, speaking French. I'm so awesome.

"Vicki, qu'est-ce que t'en penses?"

Huh? I'd been so busy congratulating myself that I had stopped listening. Damn. What were we talking about? Applications, cell phones, targets. They wanted my opinion on something.

"Ah, oui, c'est très bien. Pouvez-vous nous donner un peu plus de détail, s'il vous plaît?" Nice recovery. Compliment them and ask to hear more, that'll keep them going for a good five minutes, buying time to catch up.

Every time I thought I was awesome, someone would cut me down to size. And not in a rude way, just in a real way. Each day was a challenge and while it got easier, I was still far from fluent.

Sometimes I really longed for my yoga pants and English-filled days.

❧

The more I spoke French, the better I got. But that didn't mean I had to like it. At lunch, I usually ate by myself or went out with Marie. It's not that I wanted to be antisocial (look at my track record on the bar circuit for proof of my sociability), it's just that after hours of *problèmes* and *idées* my little brain needed a break.

I suspected people didn't really like me. But I couldn't bring myself to be "on" for the one hour of the workday I was entitled to be myself.

I'd ventured out to a few happy hours with colleagues and after several rounds of drinks everyone vowed to practice their English.

"We are so excited to speak Eengleesh wiz you!" they would shout.

Once the buzz wore off, everyone was back to speaking French, business-as-usual. I can't blame them, but it made it hard to bond. At the same time, it ensured I optimized my time in the office, then zipped home to my fiancé. It was just a job, right?

୨∘ఞ

Fall turned to winter and it became freezing-ass cold in our office. The heaters half-heartedly kicked out warm blasts of air, but a damp chill remained, making it hard to concentrate.

The bathrooms were the worst, though, because they had no direct heating. The chilly stalls were only slightly warmed by heat that had seeped in from the rest of the office. The toilet seats sent you shivering, only to be met with cold water at the sinks.

Year-round, only the cold water faucets functioned, which I doubt would even pass inspection in the United States of germaphobic America. But in the winter it was freezing cold. The water must have been 32.5 degrees Fahrenheit (that's 0.3 degrees Celsius for everyone else in the world). Seriously, if it were any colder it would be frozen. After chilling your bum off, then risking frostbite on your fingers, you had to scurry back to your desk and rub your hands together to keep warm.

How can you work like that?

Then, just when you warmed up enough to be

productive, the internet would go out. Europe in general has much faster internet speeds than North America, but that's only useful if your connection stays, well, connected.

I can't even count the number of times the internet went down. For an e-commerce company, it's kind of a big deal when the internet goes out. You would be right in the middle of updating the website and then bam! Productivity down the drain.

However, it's not like you can't find something else to do. You can always draft an email, file papers, go to the freezing cold bathroom, fill up your huge water glass, or get another coffee.

And that's just off the top of my head.

If the internet was out for, say, an hour, I could devise an even longer to-do list. Whip out that report you've been meaning to update or spruce up that power point presentation. This is a chance to do all the things you normally don't have time for because there's more important stuff to do, like check Facebook.

But everyone was gone, coats too. That could only mean one thing—smoke break. They'd taken their full packs, not just one cigarette. This was no quick nip outside, this was a mass exodus with no intention of returning anytime soon.

Maybe I'm uptight. But we're there to do a job! It's like in high school if the teacher got called out of the classroom everyone would stop working and start gossiping. But that was high school. When we were, like, fifteen. I'd never seen such a large group of so-called adults be so pumped up about getting a break.

After they'd smoked as much as they could handle, they would reluctantly return to the office, gingerly removing their coats, desperately searching for anything to do besides work. They could usually kill another 15 minutes gathered around the coffee machine, complaining about the internet being out, before they would drag their heels back to their desks.

Wouldn't time pass so much quicker if you worked?

Ah, I see it now. No wonder no one likes me. Nerd!

I've been a nerd my whole life. Always teacher's pet, thrusting my hand as high as it would go to answer every question the teacher threw out. Much like the Brazilian guy in my French orientation class, but without the promise of leaving early.

As a kid, when I wasn't jumping off roofs into pools, my head was buried in books. I'd read every Nancy Drew mystery in our school library by the time I was 8 and was thirsty for heavier material.

One day the library had a sale and I skipped lunch to buy books with my lunch money. So much to choose from! I settled on an eighth grade algebra book for $0.25. What a steal! And I even had money left for milk and cookies, the lunch of champions.

I pored over my tattered math book every day after school. Within a month I'd finished the entire book and completed my self-assigned homework. I wasn't sure yet what I'd do with this knowledge, but with engineers for parents, I wanted to do something science-y.

I often dreamed, as about 0.05% of young girls do, of being an astronaut. Sure, it would be cool to look back at Planet Earth from space. But what most allured me was being in charge of all those buttons and controls. You had to know how to handle every possible situation. Plus, you could sing "Space Oddity" and substitute your own name. "This is Major Vicki to Ground Control..."

As I got older, and watched more crime shows, I shifted my dreams toward being an FBI agent. My analytical mind was a good match for the job, and as long as my target wasn't any scarier than a soda can on a fencepost at the family farm, I was a pretty good shot.

Once I started drinking (so, twenty-one, if my mom's reading) I realized I was not cut out for a job that required such discretion. All a bad guy would have to do is ply me with a few glasses of wine and I'd blab every secret I knew. No, I needed to find a job where a drunken night of karaoke wouldn't ruin my career.

In college, I majored in mathematics partly because I loved it and partly because it made me look smart. If I had been super smart (and wanted to suffer through twelve extra credit hours) I would have gone into engineering like the rest of my family. Studying math was the easy route—it yielded a useful degree with an acceptable amount of coursework, leaving time for partying and European travel.

"You should probably choose a career path," my Greek guidance counselor recommended on one of my routine visits to his office. "What interests you?"

My dreams of being an astronaut or an FBI agent seemed silly in the face of Stavros Dostonopolous. Surely part of his job description was to steer me away from Hollywood blockbuster-type career choices.

I had one other job idea I wasn't embarrassed to admit. "Believe it or not, I like spreadsheets. I thrive on making lists and managing tasks and organizing information. I think I want to be a project manager like my mom."

"Sounds like a good use of your skills. Don't forget, though—the world could always use more teachers."

I made a face. I had nowhere near the amount of patience required to be a teacher.

"No need to make a face! You're better than you give yourself credit for. I've seen the way you grade math papers—you're a natural."

Ah yes, grading math papers. I'd picked up that part-time job at the suggestion of Stavros, who sympathized with this broke student's desire to travel the Greek islands. Every Friday I swung by the math building, saying a quick hello to my friendly advisor, then stuffed the huge stack of Math 101 papers into my satchel. Sunday night, I would pour a glass of wine, turn on The Sopranos, and attack the assignments.

The first few papers in each batch took concentration but by the tenth or so, I'd memorized the answers and grading went much quicker. When someone got the answer right, it was easy—check!

Incorrect answers were harder since I had to determine how much partial credit to give. Wanting to make math seem fun and approachable instead of scary and impossible, I was liberal with the partial credit. I marked plus signs for each part they got right and assigned an overall grade based on effort. I even invested in a pack of gold and silver star stickers, you know, like from kindergarten, and stuck them on any paper that earned a 9 or 10 out of 10. Sometimes I even wrote "Way to go" or "Rock on!" at the top. See? Nerd.

What pissed me off were the cheating cheaters who cheated. I mean, why were they even in college if they didn't want to learn? It wasn't astrophysics—it was Math 101, a basic class that was required to graduate. If this was how low they set their ambitions, maybe they should practice how to say "Would you like fries with that?" instead. And if you're gonna cheat, at least cheat off someone smart. That's Cheating 101 (a class they should probably enroll in). But most importantly, I was insulted they thought I was dumb enough to fall for it.

I'd be cruising through my papers, Tony Soprano ordering a hit on another gangster in the background, when I'd spot an answer that was clearly out of place. It would be so wrong you almost had to feel sorry for the person. I tried to give the maximum partial credit but if it's wrong, it's wrong. And they wouldn't learn if I hid their mistakes from them.

Moving on to the next paper, trying not to get

disheartened at the state of our nation's math skills, I'd hope it was a fluke. Except then I'd see the exact same error on the next paper.

Hold the phone.

There's no way that two people got it wrong in the exact same way. I'd bring back the first paper to compare, and sure enough, every single number and equation was the same. Hrm. It could have been a coincidence—maybe they both messed up at the same point and ended up with the same incorrect answer. How could I know for sure? The grading rules said that cheaters automatically got a 0 so I wanted to be certain before handing down such a harsh grade.

Upon further investigation, I'd discover my proof. The other students, the ones who'd legitimately puzzled over the answers, had pages covered in scribbles and eraser marks. But the copycats had turned in pristine sheets of paper, strongly indicating they'd copied down the answers rather than worked through them.

And given that the papers were back to back, the students likely sat next to each other in class and passed their papers in at the same time, making it even more probable that some cheating was going on, either due to proximity or because they were friends who sat next to each other.

Maybe I should have been an FBI agent after all with these amazing investigative abilities.

"No, Stavros, I don't have it in me to be a teacher. I'm so disappointed when I see the cheaters, people who clearly aren't as passionate about math as I am. And while there are always students who excel, you can't ignore the weakest students. A good teacher can handle all situations and that's not what I'm best at. I'll stick with my spreadsheets."

My mom would be so proud.

❧

Now, in my Parisian office, I had a spreadsheet open and was creating the latest test plan, this time for our mobile application. I incorporated the advice from previous tests. I spell-checked and proofread to make sure I had no typos. I emailed it to Mika so he could review my French (my poor fiancé, always paying the price for falling in love with an American girl). I saved it off as .xls, .xlsx, and .pdf.

I could complain all I wanted, but if I was going to make it, I needed to adapt.

Finally finished, I checked the time. 5:00. Sigh. Too late to send it today, everyone was already tuning out. I saved a draft in my email, deciding to send it the next day sometime between the morning coffee run and lunch. If you can't beat 'em, *rejoignez-les*.

Really, though, I had to admit I had it pretty good. I was fully integrated into the French system (hello, health care!), had a steady paycheck, and my French improved every day. My job challenged me on a daily basis. And when quittin' time rolled around, I headed home to the man of my dreams and collapsed in his arms, a brief respite before doing it again the next day.

I'd traded jammies for dresses, solitude for colleagues. It was a change, but it wasn't necessarily bad. Plus now I had lovely French paystubs to add to my dossier, should I ever move to another apartment.

And those are like pure gold over here.

30

My What a Pretty Church You Have

"I still can't believe you two are getting hitched. Didn't you just meet a few months ago?" Anne Marie asked, stacking glasses behind the Swedish Society bar.

"A *year* and a few months ago," I clarified.

"Yeah, yeah, all right. So when's the wedding?"

"We're thinking September. Nice weather and we avoid the dead summer months. Booking a venue, flowers, DJ, and the rest of it would be impossible with half the city closed. But it depends on the availability of the church. We're meeting with the priest Saturday." I sipped my champagne, anticipating her reaction.

"You? In a church?"

"Ha, I know. I *am* Catholic, I just don't go to church very often. Mika's Catholic, too." He nodded his agreement over his pint of lager.

"Too busy drinking to go to church, you are. Anyway, I agree, weddings should be in a church, all proper-like.

Where you having the reception?"

Mika and I exchanged a glance, then I turned to Anne Marie. "What about here at the Swedish Society? The location is amazing and, well, since we're regulars, maybe the price wouldn't be astronomical?"

"Yeah sure, great idea! You'll have to talk to Sonja but I'm sure she can work something out. Vicki's getting married. Good on ya!"

❧

At the crack of dawn on Saturday, we headed to our appointment with Père Nicolas. Normally sleeping off a hangover at this hour, I saw a new Paris during the five-minute walk. Store owners straightening their shops, old ladies rolling their grocery caddies, street cleaners sprucing up the sidewalks.

The 160-year-old church was nestled between typical Parisian buildings. A cobbled square with two green benches looked upon the restored façade.

According to the rules of the French Catholic Church, you have to get married in the church in your *quartier* unless you are an active member of another church. I supposed this was to avoid everyone clamoring to marry in Notre Dame or Sacré Cœur. While I have to admit it would be cool to get married in one of Paris' most famous cathedrals, this little church in the 15th *arrondissement* had its own charm.

And it was ours.

I totally wasn't envisioning gliding down the aisle in my elegant dress. Or appreciating the convenient location of the church. Or thinking how the park next door was perfect for pre-wedding photo shoots.

Or, at least I knew better than to voice those thoughts to Père Nicolas when we met him in the less-attractive administrative building next to *l'église*.

"Bienvenue." The smiling priest shook our hands. "Entrez."

We entered his spartan office. Instead of a chair, a giant exercise ball sat at his desk. You know, the ones that you think would be a good idea but you're too lazy to go out and buy, much less sit on all day? Yeah, that kind.

I glanced around for more exercise balls, not sure my abs could handle such an early morning workout. Fortunately the office also contained a lounge with armchairs and a coffee table. My abs breathed a sigh of relief.

Père Nicolas sat down, crossing his jean-clad legs. His attire contrasted with the priests of my Catholic school days, who we never saw outside of their official garb. "So, tell me a bit about yourselves and how you met."

Um, let's see. We met in a bar and we've been living together for quite some time now. We haven't been to church in ages, but your church sure is pretty!

I let Mika do the talking instead.

"Vicki is American but we met here in Paris. We've known each other for a year and a half and we're looking forward to spending the rest of our lives together."

Smooth.

Père Nicolas laid out the program, which consisted of three casual meetings with him and two sessions with other couples getting married around the same time. "Don't worry. The meetings are informal. We'll talk about marriage and faith and other doctrinal ideas. We'll also cover the logistics of the ceremony."

Mon Dieu, I hoped my French was up to the task.

"Let's begin with administration, shall we?"

My stomach dropped as he plunked a binder on the coffee table. Did stereotypical French bureaucracy extend to the Catholic Church?

"You were both baptized, yes? I will need copies of your baptism certificates."

Crikey. Contact the church I was baptized in, request a copy of my baptism certificate, request them to mail it to France, professionally translate it, deliver it to Père Nicolas. I might need to switch to only working part-time.

"If you'll just give me the name of the church, our administrative assistant will take care of the rest."

"Even for the US?" I blurted.

"Of course. We do speak a little English you know." He winked.

Holy cow! Refreshingly easy.

"We will also need a copy of your marriage license from the *mairie* before you can get married here."

Back to bureaucracy.

But I had expected this. In France, churches are only allowed to conduct the religious part of the marriage ceremony. You have to go to the *mairie*, the city hall, to be officially married. Inevitable loads of paperwork.

"Next, we need to choose a date. When were you hoping to get married?" he asked.

"September, maybe?" Only nine months away. In the US, brides booked years in advance. Considering the snail's pace of the French administration, I should have started the process a decade ago.

"Sure," he said, checking his calendar. "Which date suits you best?"

Seriously? We picked a date and everyone wrote it down, not that I was likely to forget my own wedding date. I prayed that our future meetings would go as well as this first one.

We still had a long road ahead of us.

31

Happiness

Next on the wedding to-do list: confirm the reception venue. We signed a contract with the Swedish Society *sans* hassle, as we were dealing with Swedes instead of the French.

Available on the date requested? No problem.

Free rein of the entire place? Of course!

Reasonable price, considering our menu included a five-course meal with hors d'oeuvres like reindeer carpaccio and salmon-dill canapés? It would be their pleasure.

"Are you having an open bar?" Anne Marie had her priorities straight.

"We'll have wine, champagne, and beer based on an average of five drinks per person."

"I'll go through me drinks in the first hour," she said.

"Don't worry, you can drink my mom's and the grandparents'. Trust me, there will be enough. And we can pay by the bottle if we run out."

"It's going to be weird attending the reception instead of working it."

"I know! For once you can kick back and enjoy the place. And annoy the people who *are* working."

"Exactly. You getting flowers?"

"Nah, I'm not big on flowers. Why, what do you think?"

"I'm not big on flowers either, but it would be nice to have a few arrangements. Maybe one on the piano and one in the entry. You'll have bouquets for you and the girls, right? You could order a few arrangements at the same time."

The Swedish Society was gorgeous even without flowers. Then again, a few bursts of color would personalize the décor.

It couldn't hurt to look.

❧

"How can I help you?" the florist asked without looking up from his newspaper.

"I'm looking for arrangements for my wedding. In purple, like this," I replied, pointing to a vibrant display.

"Purple?" he snorted. "You call that purple? That's not purple at all, that's dark blue."

"Dark blue? Are you sure? It seems to me—"

"If I say it's dark blue, it's dark blue." He returned to his newspaper.

I looked to Mika for help.

"We're open to suggestions," Mika said. "Anything in the blue to purple range. Could you please show us what you have?"

The florist sized Mika up, then set down the newspaper with a sigh.

"We have tulips, which can come in purple, and irises."

"Ah, tulips! Perfect. I love tulips," I chimed in.

Ignoring me, he spoke to Mika. "OK, tulips it is. When do you need them?"

"September," Mika replied.

"September? Pfft! I could be dead by then!"

"Then who would do your funeral flowers?" I wanted to ask.

The world wouldn't miss this miserable florist, that's for sure. But I didn't buy his logic. Even if he did do me the favor of expiring before my wedding date, he was an employee at a chain of florists. Surely someone else could fill the order in September, *non*?

"Come back a week before the wedding, then we'll talk. Good bye."

Dude was dreaming if he thought I would ever come back to his manky shop, much less the week before the wedding. Between welcoming out of town guests and finalizing last-minute details, no way would I have the time or desire to talk to the likes of this guy.

Of course I didn't share any of this with him as he'd already moved on to help another customer. Or, more likely, give her a lesson on color nuances and schedules.

Passing under the awning, I noticed the irony of the store's name. "Happy."

Yeah right.

>∽◆↩

Mustering up the strength for another bout of flower-hunting, we tried a mom and pop shop near the Eiffel Tower. Passionate ideas, reasonable prices. September sounded just lovely to them.

"We should have come here first," I whispered to Mika as we signed the order forms.

"Where's the fun in that? If it's not a hassle, it's not worth doing," he said.

"That should be your country's motto."

Confessions as My Single Days Come to a Close

Between working and wedding planning, I didn't have much time for writing. Or rather, between hanging out with Mika and thinking about Mika. I had really turned into a sap.

I pulled out my trusty journal, scribbled a few thoughts, and vowed to keep up the writing even after I was old and married.

I read a book, we'll call it "49 Reasons to Dislike the French," and expected to find great fodder for my own writing. Instead I found myself siding with the French on every issue. Who have I become?

I read books like that to try to feel (and look) smart. But I really prefer light, fun chick-lit. Why do people try to make you feel like it's a guilty pleasure? I can think of a lot guiltier pleasures than reading a book with a happy ending!

In a last effort to read "smart-ish" books that didn't really interest me, I considered Pride and Prejudice. I was wavering until I saw Pride and Prejudice and Zombies. The back cover states that the book "transforms a masterpiece of world literature into something you'd actually want to read." Agreed. Much like bacon, everything's better with zombies.

32

Google Search for Sanity

"At first I was afraid, I was petrified!"

Anne Marie set down her pint and wiped the foam off her lips. "Some songs just shouldn't be done in karaoke. 'I Will Survive' is tough to pull off."

I flipped the sticky pages of the song book, hesitating between George Michael and Journey. "You gotta give the girl credit, though. She's putting her heart into it."

"So, speaking of surviving, heh, how are your wedding plans going?"

"Very funny. But I see your point. All the hassle and stress is like a pre-marriage test to see if your relationship will survive. Will your partner help you out or bail?"

❧

Mika didn't strike me as the type of guy who would bail, but these were exceptional circumstances. We prepared ourselves for the worst, anticipating loads of paperwork to set the date for the civil ceremony.

We didn't even make it five minutes before hitting a roadblock.

Mika took the first stab on Google. Searching in French wasn't my strong point and navigating through government websites is a bore in any language. Page after useless page led to one conclusion: we needed to visit the *mairie* in person.

I volunteered like a pig to the slaughter. The things we do for love.

Arriving in the grand plaza of the *Mairie du 15ème* the next day, I paused to take in the scene. Impressive for a town hall in one of the less visited *arrondissements*. Built with typical Parisian cream-gray stone, the building gave the impression you might enjoy yourself once inside.

Of course that wasn't the case.

I approached the thin woman smiling from behind the information desk, grateful for the lack of a line. Quicker for the slaughter.

"Bonjour! I'm getting married and am looking for the necessary registration documents. Can you help me?"

"Of course, pas de problème. All the information is in this *dossier*." Information Desk Lady handed me a thick packet titled *Dossier du Mariage*.

How official! But this wasn't my first rodeo.

"OK, so *all* the necessary information is inside, c'est ça?"

She rolled her eyes. "Oui, mademoiselle."

Yeah, we'll see about that.

୬୭

Back at home, I worked through the *Dossier du Mariage*, item by painful item.

I ordered a copy of my birth certificate online

(remember, you need a newly issued birth certificate in case the date or location of your birth has changed) and took out a small loan to Fed-Ex the document overseas.

Next step—find an official translator for the document.[15] Following the instructions from the *dossier*, I visited the *mairie*'s website. The website told me to go to the *mairie*. I banged my head on my desk a few times, then headed back to the *mairie*.

Madame Everything-You-Need-Is-In-The-Packet greeted me at the front desk. "Bonjour! Can I help you?"

Good question. *Can* she? "Bonjour! Yes, I'm looking for the list of approved translators."

"Pas de problème," she responded, rummaging around her desk.

See? I *knew* she hadn't included everything in the packet. Maybe the "Approved Translators" file was so special it had its own *dossier*. That must be what she was looking for.

Wrong. She surfaced with a ratty piece of paper. Certainly not worthy of its own *dossier*. Hardly worth of its own space in a trash can.

"Enter this text in Google to find the list," she explained as she scrawled "cetiecap" on the paper.

"Are you freaking crazy? Why didn't you include the URL in the first place? Why give me a packet, which you insisted had all the necessary info by the way, then send me home to go to your website, which then tells me to go back to the *mairie*? At which point you tell me to go home and *Google*, for crying out loud, a website with the information I

---

[15] I know this is an official document for official purposes but it seems unnecessary to officially translate a document with only three words, the rest being numbers. The line where it says 1980? That's when I was born. The line where it says 2011? That's the year I requested the birth certificate because I'm not a one-day old baby who went back in my time machine to 1980 to request my future birth certificate. Though that gives me an idea if I decide to write French-themed sci-fi one day...

need. Does that sound normal to you? Does it? Hmm?"

That's what I wanted to say. But I also didn't want to get arrested. So instead I thanked her, like it was totally normal for city hall staff to scribble search terms on post-its as a way of disseminating official information.

Tucking the scrap in my *Dossier du Mariage*, I headed down the marble stairs. "You're lucky you're so pretty, *Mairie du 15ème*, because you are really pissing me off."

33

Stupid Hair

"That's not going to work," the *mairie* employee informed us, locks of stringy hair swinging as she tossed her head back and forth. "Nope, no way."

We were in the marriage license office, with a lady who was much less pleasant than Madame Everything-You-Need-Is-In-The-Packet from the information desk. But at least she told us straight-up that we didn't have everything we needed.

She had reviewed our *dossier du mariage*, checking items off her list, getting our hopes up that this would go smoothly.

Tax returns, check.

Proof of address, proof neither of us were currently married, proof neither of us were serial killers, check.

Sworn affidavits from our kindergarten teachers, check.

But then she stumbled on my birth certificate. The birth certificate I'd paid $30 to reissue, $70 for expedited delivery to France, and 70€ to have officially translated.

All of this to find out that it didn't have an *apostille*. Yeah, well, the stupid list didn't have an *apostille* on it either, so how was I supposed to know? I wanted to call her a million names, but as my mom taught me, if you don't have anything nice to say don't call the stringy haired bitch a stringy haired bitch.

I was feeling proud of myself for keeping my mouth shut when Stringy Haired Bitch burst my bubble. "Vous ne parlez pas français?"

Was she trying to piss me off?

There's a difference between the inability to speak French and simply not speaking French at a given point in time. I was doing the latter—choosing not to speak. Why did she assume I *couldn't* speak French? Also, did she forget that we had gone through the entire *dossier* together, in French, only two minutes earlier?

"Can you please explain to us the problem?" Mika asked with more diplomacy than she deserved. "What is an *apostille*?"

"An *apostille* is an official seal proving that a document issued by one country is official and allowed to be used by other countries. She," the lady said, pointing a finger in my general direction without deigning to look at me, "tried to submit paperwork without it and that just won't work."

No fair! She made it sound like I had snuck forged documents into my *dossier*. If an *apostille* would have been noted on the list of requirements I definitely would have obtained it.

Also, while I'm pointing fingers I have a few other people to blame. Why wasn't there an option on the birth certificate request form to add an *apostille*? America, I'm talking to you. It's the bureaucratic equivalent of "Would you like fries with that?" Upsell me. I'll buy it! I already spent nearly $200 for an expedited, translated piece of paper, so surely I would spend $50 more for a seal. But I can't do that if you don't give me the option!

And what about Miss Fancy Official Translator Pants? If the document isn't legal to be used outside of the US, then what's she doing putting her grimy little mitts on it? Couldn't she have called and said, "Didn't you mean to get an *apostille*, dummy? That'll be 50€ extra to translate." As an approved translator, she must have translated at least one American birth certificate before. I'm not the only (crazy) American girl marrying a French guy, *non*?

"Pas de problème, madame. We will get the correct document and then come back. Merci, et bonne journée."

I spit out a "bonne journée" in a tone that indicated I did not want her to have a good day at all.

A married friend of mine once enlightened me that you can't expect your partner to agree with you on everything, or even understand everything you're going through. But if he tries to get in your boat, you're off to a great start. And at a minimum, if you're complaining about someone and he doesn't quite understand the problem, he can at least point out that the person you're complaining about has stupid hair. Wise woman, this friend.

My blood was boiling as we descended the stupid steps of the *mairie*.

"I can't believe I have to go through this hassle again! Why didn't they include the *apostille* in the blasted *Dossier du Mariage* that they assured me contained everything I needed? And why did she have to be such a bitch? I speak French, lady! Here's some French for you—*ferme ta gueule!*"

"Plus she had stupid hair," Mika added.

See why I'm marrying this guy?

34

Fuchsia Lipstick

"Hello?" I answered my cell phone, rushing to an empty conference room and shutting the door. I generally didn't answer personal calls at work but since I didn't recognize the phone number, it might be important.

OK, no, I was just curious but I was sure it would only take a minute.

"Oui, allô? It's the *Mairie du 15ème*. We have the pleasure to inform you the date for your wedding has been set."

I crossed my fingers, hoping it would be sometime near the end of September, which was what we'd requested but were given no guarantee.

"Le date est le 23 septembre, 2011. That works for you?"

"Oui!" Though I was half-tempted to say no, just to see what she would say. They won't change the date so why do they ask? "No, actually, there's a Golden Girls marathon on TV that day. Can we reschedule?"

Good thing I didn't say half of what came to mind. My life was hard enough.

"On behalf of the *Mairie du 15ème*, congratulations and we wish you a wonderful day."

After weeks of drowning in birth certificates and translations and *apostilles*, it felt damn good to receive the call. It was official. I was getting married.

ক্ষৈ৶

I slipped back to my desk and worked until lunch. Once everyone else left the office, I ate at my desk and browsed bridesmaids dresses online. I already had my own gown but needed to pick out the dresses for my bridal party.

The bridal party contained three girls and three guys. I'd chosen my sister-in-law, Nikki, my soon-to-be sister-in-law, Adeline, and a friend, who we'll just call Maid of Honor[16]. For the guys, Mika chose two of his good friends, Charles and Etienne, plus my brother.

Six attendants is about average these days. Some American weddings have up to twenty, but if I did that there wouldn't be anyone left to fill the church pews.

In the US, the bridal party has some sort of unity to their attire. Bridesmaids often wear the same style and

---

[16] I considered calling her She Who Must Not Be Named but even that gives her more notoriety than she deserves. I won't delve into it because I have my hands full complaining about French bureaucracy, but let me just give a little advice. If someone asks you to be in their wedding but you don't want to for whatever reason (you don't actually like said person as much as they think you do or you're too busy with your career/boyfriend/whatever) do everyone a favor and tell that person *before* you're plastered all over their wedding album for the rest of their lives. One honest conversation can save a lot of disappointment down the road. And you can avoid being called She Who Must Not Be Named. Unless that's what you're going for.

color of dress. You'll occasionally see the same color on different styles of dress or the same cut of dress in a small range of coordinating colors. When I was a bridesmaid in Stephen's wedding the previous year, Nikki requested I wear a turquoise dress but left the style up to me. That way I didn't have to squeeze my booty into an unflattering one-size-fits-no-one style. Isn't she thoughtful?

While the concept of matching attire seems normal to Americans, the French find it bizarre. I realized how foreign my concept was after numerous internet searches turned up nil. One initially promising site, I kid you not, featured a picture of suspiciously young Asian girls sewing dresses. Thanks, but I'd rather not support a sweatshop.

Lunch hour was half over and I hadn't found a single Parisian bridal boutique with more than one dress in the same color. Even by accident it seems they should have a few dresses in the same color.

Maybe they didn't post everything online? Possible, but not efficient. So, yeah, very possible for a French store.

I clicked over to a popular American wedding apparel website that lets you play with paper dolls (well, virtual dolls) to visualize the dresses on your bridesmaids. You can even change their hair color and give them a tan.

My coworkers trickled in as I put the finishing touches on my miniature party. I needed to get back to work before anyone spotted my computer screen. Damn. My mini bridal party was trapped on an American website.

How was I going to find dresses in Paris, and affordable ones at that?

ɚ⚫ɚ

"A street near Barbès-Rochechouart has a ton of bridal stores," Mika announced that night over dinner. "Want to check it out this weekend?"

I made a face. "That part of town is so dodgy."

"I know, but it's the only place we'll find more than one dress in the same color. At least we know it's affordable. They can't charge a fortune in that neighborhood."

Bless him! He was already proving to be infinitely more helpful than Maid of Honor. "Sure, let's go. Thanks for your help."

ভঞ্জ

Website printouts in hand, we arrived at the first store. "Bonjour! We're looking for bridesmaids dresses, something along the lines of these?"

The plump saleslady smiled. A splash of fuchsia on her teeth matched her lips. "Yes, yes! Right this way!" Her English was flavored with a thick Eastern European accent.

"You like this?" She held up a hot pink number drowning in sequins. "This is great one. We have other beautiful dress, fancy."

I couldn't wait to see her idea of fancy.

She sifted through a nearby rack and pulled out another blinding gown. "Like mermaid, this one."

The long sea blue dress shimmered in the fluorescent light. It did look like it could swim away, if that's what she meant.

"Do you have any with fewer sequins? And any in dark purple?"

She snorted. "Fewer sequin? Is wedding, no? This means sequin! But OK, yes, for you, I find dress with no sequin." She winked as she sashayed to the back room.

Were we conspiring? Were non-sparkly dresses illegal? Did I need a special favor for a dress that didn't give off its own phosphorescence?

"This is only one I have," she said, thrusting a lavender satiny number in my arms and steering me towards the changing room. "Try on, you will like."

I tried it on, even though I wasn't the same size as any of my bridesmaids and the color was wrong. But I feared what Fuchsia Lips would do if I refused.

The watery color made my skin look green, and the cheap fabric was already ripping at the seams. As I was about to take it off, she flung the curtain of the dressing room open for the whole store to see.

"Beautiful. You see? Is what I said. Very beautiful. You buy?"

I considered her question. What if she forced me into each of her sparkly numbers until I claimed to find one I liked? I could be pulling sequins out of my ears for weeks. I had to get out of there.

"Um, I need to think about it. But thank you."

Mika and I attempted a few more stores, all with the same result. Gross dresses, and none in the right color.

"I need a drink," I sighed, spotting a café on the corner.

Over a couple of beers we laughed about our adventure. But I still had no dresses. "Clearly we're not going to find what we want on this street. Am I going to have to order my dresses from the sweatshop?"

"What?!?" He nearly spit out his beer.

Guess I didn't tell him about that one.

"Or I can order from the American website and Mom can bring them. It's a lot to pack for an overseas flight and the girls can't try them on first, but maybe it could work."

Mika's eyes glazed over. "Mm-hmm."

"Don't worry, I'll figure it out. You've already helped more than a groom should have to. Thanks, sweetie."

"Hey, if you reward me with beer, I'll do pretty much anything."

"I'll remember that, hubby."

35

Wedding Cake and Tummyaches

"Chocolate with buttercream frosting, white cake with raspberry filling, and, oh, I seem to have forgotten a flavor. I'll be right back."

Mika and I sat on leopard-print bar stools in a cake shop we'd found online. Palm fronds from the world's fakest indoor plant tapped my shoulder. While not the chic Parisian bakery of my dreams, it didn't have chic Parisian prices either. I brushed the leaves away, calculating how many more bottles of champagne my guests could enjoy if we purchased our cake here.

The baker pushed through the swinging door and set a sample of banana cream frosting on the tray, which already contained six different cakes and eleven flavors of frosting. The combinations were endless![17]

"Sample as many combinations as you wish and note

---

[17] Or, for those counting along, 72. Close enough to endless!

the ones you like best. Take your time! I'll come check on you in a bit."

A kid in a candy shop, or rather an adult in a tropical cake shop, I started shoveling cake combinations in my mouth. Three samples in, I caught Mika's eye.

"What?" I said, lowering my apish arm to a more dainty position.

"Nothing," he said, picking up a piece of hazelnut cake and spreading it with French silk frosting. "I just think... well... I know she said we could sample as much as we wanted but considering we haven't eaten lunch yet, you might get a stomach ache if you eat too much."

"OK, Mom, I'll take it easy," I replied, deciding I could skip the fruit ones. That eliminated 24 combinations, leaving me with a reasonable 48. The pieces were small. I'd be fine.

Mika smiled and shook his head as he popped the sample in his mouth.

"Have you found any pairings you like?" The baker had returned a little while later with a notepad.

Wiping my mouth, I racked my brain to remember the distinct flavors. They were all so good!

"Chocolate cake with buttercream frosting was my favorite," Mika offered. "The Madagascar vanilla was tasty, too."

"Yes," I mumbled, swallowing the last of my bite. "Both sound good."

"Shall we fill out the order form? You'll need to select the style of the cake and the accent color."

"Great! Wonderful! Let's do the three-tiered cake— that's good for 80 people, right? And here's a color sample of the shade of purple we're using! And we'd like this design here!" I pointed to the least gaudy design in their catalogue.

Mika and the baker shared a glance.

"So... I think I ate too much cake. I'm on a sugar high.

Sorry! It was too tasty!"

The baker laughed and completed the order form. My sugar rush was wearing off and a bellyache was setting in.

Why was Mika always right?

"Do you mind if I step outside for some air?" I slid off the stool and wobbled towards the door. "Can you handle the rest?"

A few minutes later, Mika emerged from the bakery, stuffing the receipt in his wallet. "All taken care of. And good news—delivery is only 35€ and their delivery hours are 10 am to 6 pm, so that works with the timing of our reception. I told her we'd like it there between 2 pm and 4 pm."

"Great, thanks!" I stood on my tiptoes to give him a kiss, but then felt a bit woozy. "So, what do you say we grab some lunch?"

"Sounds good. What are you in the mood for? Cake?"

36

Bachelorette Party

"L'enterrement de vie de jeune fille," literally "the burial of the young girl's life." Morbid, much? The Brits are more optimistic than the French with "hen parties" (if you're confused, remember "hen" is like "chick").

As an American, I like the straightforward "bachelorette party." No one's dying, no one's turning into an animal. At least not if everything goes well.

"Right then, I'll fill these up straight away."

Anne Marie hadn't even sat down before sliding three empty pitchers off the table with the ease of someone who's been tending bar for years. The rest of us girls settled in around the rustic wooden table while Ammo headed to the self-serve barrels of wine. Clearly the reason we had chosen the kitschy medieval-themed restaurant.

"I've never been here before," Chris said. "How does it work?"

The waiter came on cue and deposited an overflowing

basket of veggies on the table. He set three crocks of mayonnaise around the basket.

"Welcome! Eat as many veggies as you like! Then help yourself to the all-you-can eat buffet of charcuterie. I'll come back for your meat order. Bon appétit!"

Wooster's eyes widened. "I've never heard of an all-you-can-eat restaurant in France."

"And that's not all," I said. "There's a cheese platter and dessert as well. Eat up! We need to counteract all the alcohol we're about to consume."

Anne Marie returned, sloshing red wine as she set the pitchers down. She poured everyone a glass, then Marie stood up to toast. "I'm used to seeing the serious side of Vicki at work. So let's toast to a wild night! To the girls! Cheers!"

My goal was to have a memorable evening with good friends. I detest the notion of squeezing in "one last bit of fun" before getting married as if marriage is going to be no fun at all. As if this was my last chance to do what I wanted before having to get my plans approved by my husband. I partied now, I would party once I was married. I hung out with the girls now, I would hang out with the girls once I was married.

I'd toast to that.

"Before I forget," Maid of Honor chimed in, "you have to wear this." She pulled a fluffy feather boa from her bag.

"I'd be delighted." I wrapped it elegantly around my neck, or as elegant as a red feather boa can be. "Can this evening get any classier?"

As if in response, a costumed bard entered the dining hall singing, "When the moon hits your eye, like a big-a pizza pie, that's amore." The tune bounced off the stone walls creating quite the cacophony. Or maybe that was just Ondine, my gorgeous fashion designer friend, and me singing along.

We laughed, we sang. We plowed through course after

course, pitcher after pitcher, until we were stuffed to the brim.

"Whaddya say? One more pitcher of wine or should we move on?"

As we contemplated Anne Marie's question, the bard strummed the first notes of "La Cucaracha."

"Let's go," we said in unison.

Of course, it didn't stop us from chanting along as the nine of us filed out the door.

∾⚮∾

"Next up, Harry's Bar," Maid of Honor announced. Former haunt of Ernest Hemingway and other famous Paris-dwellers, the wood-paneled bar features rambunctious decor and lively, largely expat clientele. It's the birthplace of the Bloody Mary and the Side Car. Stick that bit of trivia in your pocket and save it for later. You'll thank me at your next pub quiz.

"At these prices, the drinks better be the best I've ever had," Fanny[18] said, brushing her stylish bangs out of her way-too-pretty-to-be-so-nice face.

No sooner had our waiter slid 150€ worth of cocktails on the table, ice cubes still clanking in their glasses, did I start harassing the pianist to play "Moon River." I mean, *requesting* him to.

Piano Man put up a fight but his resistance was futile. Hell hath no fury like a drunken girl at her bachelorette

---

[18] Let's get this out of the way now (I'm talking to you, Anne Marie, who I know is giggling at this very moment). Fanny is an ordinary, if not common, name in French. In American English, you might meet someone named Fannie, but more likely if you hear "fanny" you think they're talking about someone's rear-end. In British English, "fanny" refers to, well, their "front-end." So imagine Anne Marie's squeals when I said "You have to meet my co-worker, she's the best. I love Fanny!"

party in the mood to sing.

As he began to play, I shouted along. "Moon river, wider than a mile..." Wait, was it "mile" or "smile?" "Mile" makes more sense but something's telling me "smile." Crap, now I missed the whole first verse.

The song sped along, just out of my reach. I didn't catch up until the final glorious line. "Moooooooooooon river... aaaaaaaaaaaaaaand meeeeeeeeeeeeeeeeee."

Piano Man twisted his face in a familiar grimace. "All that hassle for *that?*" He shook his head in an effort to clear it of my annoying existence.

"Ready for the next bar?" Maid of Honor asked.

Slurping the last *centime* of our world-famous drinks, we deposited the tumblers on the table and clamored across the street to Footsie.

Footsie is a theme bar that plays on the idea of the French Stock Exchange (FTSE, hence the name) where the price of drinks fluctuates depending on current popularity.

But that night (and incidentally, the only other night I'd been there) the menu boards weren't working so all the drink prices were set at the max. No gimmick plus we got to pay full price. Or rather, my *amis* got to pay full price since they treated me the entire evening.

"What'll you have?" Chris asked.

Given how much I was sloshing back, I was concerned for my friends' budgets. My liver wishes I'd show the same concern. *Shhh, liver. We're having a good time here.*

"Vodka cranberry, please."

I drummed my fingers on the edge of the bar while the bartender slowly filled a cup with ice. On the best of days, I start out with a minus 2 in patience. Once the drinking sets in, I'm closer to negative infinity. *How long is this guy going to take?* What a buzz kill.

He left me no choice but to hop on the bar. This girl needed to sing! To the world!

The barstool disagreed.

As my too-high heel struck the bottom rung, I crashed before my show could begin. Instant bruise.[19] Dusting myself off I looked around for my friends. Thankfully none had witnessed the embarrassing fall. Then again, if they'd been around, they probably wouldn't have let me climb on the bar in the first place. *Where are they?*

My shin throbbed. As the bartender finally served my drink, I realized what I needed. "Excuse me, I'd like four shots of tequila, too. Thanks."

The bar was sweltering as drunken crowds pushed against me. *Where is everyone?* They'd likely gone out for some air, but surely they'd be back soon. I didn't know who'd be in the mood for shots or who was even left at this point, but I figured four was a good calculation.

This time the bartender was speedy and before I'd even gotten halfway through my drink, he splashed the shots on the bar along with salt and limes.

Crap.

The crowd kept pushing in around me. I wouldn't be able to save my space at the bar for long, and a stray arm was bound to knock the glasses over before my friends got back. There was no way I could carry the shots and the salt and limes through the crowd without spilling them, but there was no way I'd let that much alcohol go to waste.

Only one option remained. I had to take one for the team. Or, more precisely, four.

Word to the wise. If faced with this decision, take any other option than the one I took. Donate the shots to charity, make new friends to share them with, or leave

---

[19] This bruise lasted for over a year. That's hard core. To honor the French's love for a pun, I was bad to the bone. Here's a tomato. Throw it at me—I deserve it.

them sad and alone on the bar. But do not drink four shots when you've already had way too much to drink. In fact, don't drink four shots in one night. Period. Just don't.

"There you are!" Fanny, Clare, and Chris approached, wiping the sweat from their brows.

"We thought you were coming with us outside. It's burning up in here," Clare said.

Clare was another friend I'd met from volunteering. She lived in my neighborhood and was going to regret that soon, considering she'd likely have to escort me home.

"Are those our shots?" Fanny asked, eyeing the four empty glasses on the bar.

"They were. I think I might have made a mistake." Understatement of the year.

Next thing I knew, the room was spinning. Uh oh.

"Time to go," Clare said. "Let me round up the others and we'll head to the taxi stand."

❦

Waiting for a taxi in Paris can be painful. Waiting for a taxi at 2 in the morning is excruciating.

First, there aren't many taxis on the road that late at night. Even though it's when people are most desperate for a ride (since public transportation has stopped running) taxi drivers don't want to work the late shift. They want a 9 to 5 job like everyone else. Well, dummies, if we're all working from 9 to 5 then we don't need to take a stupid taxi!

Second, there are some unsavory types waiting for taxis at that hour. Drunks, douchebags, drunken douchebags. They cut in line, they puke on the sidewalk, they get in fights.

Makes my singing look like a night at the opera in comparison.

When it's finally your turn and the last taxi on earth appears on the horizon, you think you're saved. Until the guy pulls up and asks where you're going. "To the 15th arrondissement," you'd say, about to open the door.

"Nope, sorry, not going that way," he'd snap, rolling the window up before you'd even realized what happened.

How could he "not be going my way?" He's a taxi! His job is to go my way! What is this, Taxi Roulette? You flag down a taxi and let him take you wherever he was already planning on going and hope that it'll be close to where you're going?

As you inhaled his exhaust fumes, you'd realize what a jerk he had truly been. Not only did he blow you off for an insane reason, but he'd left you stranded in the middle of the night.

৩০৫৬

"The winner takes it all!" I wailed. "The winner takes it all. The winner takes it all! The winner takes it ALLLLLLLLLLLLLL!"

I couldn't remember the lyrics to my favorite ABBA song so, to the listening pleasure of my fellow taxi line waiters, I sang the same line for all the verses. As you do.

I assume my friends paid the bill before shuffling me outside. I only remember holding Fanny's hand at the taxi stand and waiting for what simultaneously felt like a lifetime and only five seconds.

Everyone must have been praying for a taxi to come and take me away, because just as I was about to launch into "Dancing Queen," a cab sped up and screeched to a halt.

Leaving a trail of red feathers in my wake, a sad boa drooping from my neck, I tumbled into the taxi. Clare scooted in after me and gave the driver my address.

I snuggled into her lap and started counting prime numbers. 1, 2, 3, 5... then all of a sudden we were home. Oh thank God.

Heaving myself out of the taxi, I mustered the energy to clunk up all five flights of stairs, glancing at the 3rd floor as a potential bed. *Nah, I can make it. I think.*

"Welcome home, honey!" Mika greeted.

I rushed past him to the bathroom to throw up.

"Hi honey," I shouted from behind the door. "I'll be out in, um, well, in a bit."

"Take your time."

Ah, true love.

37

His Turn

"You look ridiculous. Have a great time!"

One week after my singing/bar-climbing/vomiting party in celebration of my last days as a single lady, my husband-to-be set out for his bachelor party.

While my party had American flair, spiced with my particular flavor of fun—too much drinking—Mika had a traditional French party. That is to say, totally dorky because the bachelor wears a ridiculous costume.

American bachelorettes might wear feather boas (I did) or penis necklaces (I threatened death to anyone who even tried). In France, they get the biggest kick out of dressing the leading lady or man in the stupidest costume they can find, then parading them around town all day drinking half pints of beer. I've seen guys in Raggedy Ann costumes or generic wig-and-dress drag, always with chest hair poking out. Girls usually wear a dumpy disguise, like a full body dinosaur suit or an Easter bunny.

As evidenced by my own bachelorette party, I don't need such gimmicks to make a fool of myself. Just a round of shots.

But this wasn't my party so it wasn't my call.

Mika's best man, Charles, had labored over the costume all week. Whipping it out of the bag, Mika's face turned from excitement to horror in a nanosecond.

"Superman? You've got to be kidding me."

"SuperMIKA," Charles corrected. The shirt emblazoned with the iconic logo sported an "M" instead of the usual "S." "You've got speedo undies and red boots, too. The whole get-up. You're welcome."

I got the camera ready while Mika dressed. He marched out of the bedroom in full regalia. Man, those speedos were tight.

Ever the good sport, Mika strutted his stuff out of the apartment, leaving red footprints behind.

I settled in for a sober evening at home, still queasy at the thought of drinking after the weekend before. I dozed off around midnight, cradling the phone in case my fiancé called. He wasn't as big a drinker as I was, plus the guys would be buying him drinks all day.

It could get ugly.

My ringtone startled me out of my sleep. "Hi honey." I rubbed my eyes and sat up.

"Heeeeeeeeey, babe! I'm just callin' to say everything's good. I drank water, like you said, and only took a few shots, like you said. Everything is sooooooo great. I love you! Be home soon!"

Uh oh. This could only mean one thing. He was shit-faced. As I well knew, anytime someone who's been drinking says "Everything's great" it means they're three sheets to the wind and five minutes away from puking.

I poured a huge glass of water and waited until I heard the familiar sounds of a drunk person making their way up five flights of stairs. Familiar because that had been me a week earlier.

I opened the door as he arrived on the landing.

"Heeeeeeeeeeeey, honey!"

"Hi sweetie," I said, shoving the glass in his hands. "Come in and drink this water, then we're gonna get you to bed."

He chugged the water while I took in his outfit. He'd lost the cape, and the original black hue of his boots peeked through splotches of red paint. But hey, he'd kept it on all day. I had to give him credit for that.

"Would you like a bite to eat?"

"Umm... uh oh." Before he could respond he dashed to the bathroom and threw up. From the sounds of it, I'd have to send a clean-up crew in after him (meaning, me).

I should have been mad—I mean, who wants to clean up someone else's puke in the middle of the night?—but I was relieved. Payback! Mika had cleaned up my after-party mess without saying a word. Which sounds great but I had been feeling guilty about it. Now here was my golden opportunity to pay him back.

"Sorry about that," he said, opening the bathroom door.

"No problem, sweetie! Let's get you tucked into bed and I'll take care of it."

In sickness and in health, in good times and in bad. Yeah, I think we were ready.

38

Deliver Me

As the RSVPs rolled in, we counted a nice-sized group for our wedding, with a happy mix of family and friends coming from the US and all corners of France.

For the out-of-towners, I planned a week's worth of activities that everyone could either participate in or ignore in favor of their own activities. I didn't want anyone to be bored but I didn't want to be bossy either. Well, I did want to be bossy but I didn't want anyone to know I wanted to be bossy.

And so the Wedding Welcome Packet was born.

Between infuriating appointments at the *mairie* and hair-pulling visits to florists, I drafted a guide with maps for each event and tips for what to wear/bring/etc. I didn't want guests showing up in ball gowns or shorts unless necessary (and probably not at the same event).

"Dad! How was your flight?" I hugged him, then enveloped my step-mom in a bear hug. We were in the lobby of their hotel, with Mika, Stephen, and Nikki in tow.

"Good, good. Here are those boxes of mac and cheese you asked for. So what's the plan for this evening?"

"Didn't you read the Wedding Welcome Packet?"

"Uh... yeah. Of course. But it's buried in my suitcase. Mind giving me a refresher?"

I cut him a little slack. He did just deliver what he thought was a year's supply of mac and cheese (at twenty boxes, he wasn't even close). Leafing through my own beat-up packet, I reminded everyone we'd be having a casual dinner near the hotel.

We strolled through the neighborhood, my family enjoying the exotic (to them) sights while I ran through a mental checklist of wedding plans.

"Crap! Mika, we need to confirm the delivery time with the cake shop. They said they could deliver from 10 to 6 but the Swedish Society said no one will be on site until 3:00. I'm sure I'm overreacting but do you mind calling real quick?"

"Sure, no problem. I'm with you—I don't trust them. Scheduling the delivery was suspiciously simple."

Thankful for smartphones, he found the shop's phone number and gave them a ring. From the snippets of conversation I overheard, it wasn't going well.

"I know you said we didn't need to check... between 3 pm and 6 pm... well it's because they're not open before then... available from 10 am to 6 pm... I don't understand the problem...."

Then it clicked.

Mika and I turned to each other as we suddenly understood what their careless wording meant. Much like the cable guy who says he'll come between 8 am and 8 pm, the cake delivery people promise to deliver your cake sometime between 10 am and 6 pm. But you can't specify a time within that range. You're entirely at their mercy

Which was a place I could not afford to be.

"What is their plan? They're just going to leave the cake on the Swedish Society's doorstep? Is this the first time they've encountered this problem? Every other wedding they've ever done was held at a venue staffed round the clock that could accept delivery at all hours?" Add in a few more expletives and you'll have the rant I spewed at Mika while he tried to salvage the situation.

Covering the mouthpiece of the phone, he said, "It's 'absolutely impossible' for us to set a time and 'absolutely impossible' for them to know where they will be at any given time on Saturday."

His emphasis on "absolutely impossible" indicated the words came directly from the absolutely impossible people on the other end of the line.

How did they have no idea where they would be? Do they just load up the cakes and drive, periodically checking their location and hoping it matches where they need to be? They should organize the delivery list to avoid zigzagging across town all day. How about adding a slight layer of complexity and delivering our cake later in the day? They could deliver all the cakes for children's birthday parties and christenings in the morning, then swing around with the wedding cakes.

Isn't it more likely that children's events are earlier in the day and weddings are later? Or do they simply not care?

"Here's your cake, kid. Sorry your birthday party ended three hours ago. Maybe next time your parents can order from a real company."

The logistics surely aren't impossible. I'll give you "kind of difficult" and "might require functioning brain cells" but I will not accept "absolutely impossible."

Fortunately, ever-calm Mika worked out a deal.

They agreed to "help us out" and "take care of everything." All we needed to do was come into the shop at some point during the week (time? I have tons of it!) and do a back-alley-style cash transaction where we would give them 83€ in an envelope marked Rip-Off Delivery, Inc., which they would then hand over to a third-party delivery service who could guarantee delivery on Friday. The bakery would issue us a check to refund the 35€ we had paid for their in-house delivery.

Piece of cake!

I don't know why they didn't propose the other delivery service in the first place or at least earlier in the phone call. And I'm not sure it qualified as "taking care of everything" when it still involved multiple steps on our end.

"Who's ready for dinner? I'm famished."

Copious amounts of wine and reminiscing with the family eased me into a relaxed mood. But I still had a nagging feeling about this blasted cake.

39

Picnics in Paradise

As the week wore on and more guests arrived, I chilled out. The weather was cooperating, people were enjoying themselves, and my Wedding Welcome Packet was proving mighty helpful.

Could it really be going this well? Would everything go this smoothly on the big day?

"How about this spread?" my dad asked, beaming with pride.

The Wednesday before the wedding, we gathered for a picnic at the Eiffel Tower. Laid out before us was a feast worthy of the history books. Cheese and *charcuterie* and baguettes and wine reached as far as the eye could see. Or at least to the edge of the picnic blanket.

"You found everything OK?"

"The Wedding Welcome Packet clearly stated how to get here and where the nearest grocery store was," Dad replied with a wink. "And the picture of the Eiffel Tower was a nice touch."

"You joke but I know you like it. Well, what are we waiting for? Dig in!"

Over *pâté* and *foie gras*, my friends and family shared stories of their trip so far. Some language barriers, a few issues with directions, but for the most part everything was going well.

The picnic was a success, too. I'd prepared for Wedding Week with care, ensuring our lunch locale was one of the few parks that allowed picnics. Camped in front of the *Tour Eiffel*, we were surrounded by numerous groups on the grassy lawn engaging in the same behavior as us. It was a safe bet.

Which seems normal—you meet in a park and everyone eats. What could go wrong?

৩৯৯৫

French park rangers, that's what. I can't even count the number of times I've been shooed away from picnicking by these bottom-rung authority figures.

Marie and Fanny and I occasionally lunch at a park near our office. One time I brought a salad and dared to eat it with a fork while sitting on the lawn. Salad. Fork. Lawn.

I'm downright despicable.

"Ma'am, I'm going to have to ask you to leave," said a park ranger as he crossed his arms.

"Me?" I asked. I spotted two teenagers passing a joint, a middle-aged man flicking a cigarette butt, and an old lady chatting with a friend while her dog took a dump in the grass. "What am I doing wrong?"

"Picnics are not allowed. You need to leave."

I would hardly call eating a salad a picnic. Was it because I was sitting on the grass? Cigarette butts and dog butts are permitted, but not human butts? Although, now

VICKI LESAGE

that I thought about it, why did I even want to sit on this foul grass?

"What if I sit on a bench?" I gestured toward two girls eating sandwiches on a nearby bench.

"No picnics. No forks, no containers. Sandwiches are tolerated. And you can sit on the lawn. But no picnics."

So the main thing turning my lunch into a picnic was my fork? If I dumped my salad onto some bread then it would pass. Was he worried I wasn't eating enough carbs? Was he on the Anti-Atkins squad? Or the French Baker's Union?

"OK, we'll leave. Sorry," I mumbled, not at all OK with it nor planning to leave nor really even sorry. The ranger must have suspected my insincerity so he hovered until I stood up and actually left.

"Just so you know, I have the power to give you a fine for picnicking," he warned, shaking a finger at me. "Let's not let this happen again."

Trust me, it wouldn't happen again. If I learned one lesson from this, it's to never eat a salad for lunch.

ॐ

"I can't believe we ate *everything*," my mom remarked.

Empty packages and full bellies. The picnic was a hit. No intruding park rangers, no guilt-ridden secret-salad-eating. My friends and family enjoyed a picnic unscathed by French rules and regulations.

"And drank everything, too," my dad said, emptying the last drops of wine from his plastic cup.

It was almost a shame to not have anything to complain about. Almost.

40

Tomorrow Is Only a Day Away

Tomorrow. Tomorrow I'll be married. Soon the days of stumbling home from bars like a drunken fool would be gone. I'd have my loving husband to escort me, thus eliminating the stumbling.

I kind of had two days left, since the church wedding was on Saturday. While the civil ceremony on Friday would mark the official debut of our marriage, for me the true wedding was when I'd walk down the aisle in my fancy schmancy dress.

According to the Wedding Welcome Packet, which I'd now memorized *par cœur*, Thursday was the rehearsal dinner. Out of town guests, the wedding party, and our parents (so, a good chunk of our guest list) would be dining at none other than Refuge des Fondus.

American rehearsal dinners serve two purposes. One, it's a way to feed the masses after they've rehearsed their roles for the big day. The wedding party meets at the church, practices what they'll say, who walks down the aisle when, and so forth. The other purpose is to give the soon-to-be-united families a chance to meet in case they haven't already. Out-of-towners are thrown in the mix because it'd be rude to let them have any fun that doesn't center around the bride and groom. At least they score a free meal.

As I'd grown up with this tradition, I considered it normal. Sure, you're throwing a huge wedding and feeding everyone and have a million details to plan, so why not do a smaller-scale version the day before?

There's a reason weddings are a billion dollar industry in the US.

"What!" Père Nicolas exclaimed. "I mean, no, we do not have rehearsals. You walk down the aisle when the music begins and we read from the Wedding Ceremony Packet. Don't worry, it will go smoothly."

Worry? No need to worry anymore—I'd found my long-lost twin, one who shared my enthusiasm for wedding packets.

"Thank you, Père Nicolas. I'm a bit lost between the two cultures and don't want to offend anyone by leaving out important traditions."

He smiled. "You can still have the rehearsal dinner if you want, of course."

We probably should have simply called it "dinner" but then it wouldn't have felt so wedding-y.

So the evening before the wedding, forty of us packed into the cozy fondue restaurant, which Mika and I had reserved for the entire night. Guests clambered over the tables, bumping heads on the ceiling and knees on the wall. The always-wonderful wait staff deposited baby bottles of wine in front of everyone.

"Toast, toast!" the crowd chanted.

Never one to be bashful, I addressed my friends and family with an impromptu speech.

"Six years ago I moved to the lovely city of Paris. I

found this restaurant and called it my home. I've been here more times than I can remember, likely because I never leave with a sober hair on my head."

My dad laughed, while my mom had that worried look moms are known for.

"But suffice it to say, " I continued, "I have nearly 200 wonderful dinners to remember this place by. This restaurant represents everything I love about Paris. In fact, the only thing I love more than melted cheese and wine in baby bottles, is my wonderful husband-to-be. So, drink up and let's celebrate!"

I was giddy. The wedding would soon be here, I was surrounded by the people I loved, and I had a night of wine-in-baby-bottle drinking ahead of me.

Life was good.

Almost too good. Would it crash down any moment now? Years of living in this beautiful yet frustrating city taught me to always be on the lookout for the next catastrophe.

∽∾

Squinting at the sun's reflection off the pristine limestone steps of the *mairie* the next day, I counted my lucky stars for the gorgeous weather. A city normally dressed in gray was bright and beautiful before my eyes.

Lovely day to get married.

I straightened Mika's tie, not because it needed it, but because it seemed the thing to do. "Ready?" I croaked. My vocal cords had taken a beating at the rehearsal dinner (I challenge you to get through a night of wine in baby bottles without singing your heart out) and I had somehow twisted my ankle (again, I blame the wine) but I was as ready as I was ever going to be.

"Can't wait."

We marched up the stairs and into the lobby, where

our family had already arrived (thank the wedding packet for that). After a paparazzi-style stream of photos with every possible combination of family members, we mounted the red-carpeted staircase and entered an elegant chamber.

Two ornate wooden chairs with plush burgundy seats waited for us, surrounded by rows of slightly more austere versions of the same chair for our guests. They really pulled out all the stops for a civil ceremony!

A panel of French bureaucrats lined the front of the room. The Enemy. Masters of delayed paperwork and disgruntled grunts.

Yet the faces smiling back at me softened my hardened heart. Their formal yet friendly stance gave the impression that they were truly honored to perform our wedding service.

In the center of the panel stood the *Adjoint au Maire du 15ème* (that's the assistant to the mayor), decorated in a red, white, and blue sash that was a handsome version of the one Miss America wears. Count on the French to pull off pompous attire without being pretentious. Could you imagine if *I* tried to wear a sash like that?

"Welcome everyone. Please take your seats as we celebrate this momentous occasion," the *adjoint* boomed.

As he ran through the official-speak, he added charming touches resulting in a flowery speech that felt French and warm. Not the frigid civil ceremony I'd been expecting. Particularly not after the bureaucratic hell I'd gone through to get to that point. Stacks of papers and grating *rendez-vous* fell to the wayside as I reveled in the moment.

"Do you take this man…"

Whoa, better pay attention here! I almost missed the most important part. "Oui," I declared.

"And do you take this woman…"

Wow, it's happening. In one minute I'm going to be…

"Oui."

Married. You know, it's funny but I actually felt the transformation from being single to being married.

"Madame Lesage?" Mika asked.

Madame! That had a nice ring to it. "Yes, Monsieur Lesage?"

"Ready for champagne?"

"You bet."

❦

Rows of champagne flutes greeted our guests as we crammed into our apartment. We were saving the big hurrah for the church ceremony and reception the next day, but still wanted to celebrate our official marriage with our family.

The pop of the champagne cork was music to my ears. Bureaucracy behind me, married life in front of me.

I was ready to celebrate!

And so were my guests. We plowed through quite a few bottles of champagne, nibbled on hors d'œuvres, and gave our new Wii (a wedding present from my office) a workout.

The party was in full swing when the phone rang.

"Oui, allô? It's the cake shop calling and I have some terrible news and I'm talking too fast for you to understand," the woman at the end of the line said. The sun glinted off my champagne glass, reminding me that karma exists. I may have nice weather, but I still have bullshit to deal with.

"One moment, ma'am," I cooed. I passed the phone to Mika and mouthed "Help, please!" then returned to my guests before he had a chance to say no. As a good wife does.

Wii-boxing with my dad, I tried not to listen in on the cake conversation. But Mika's expression had me worried.

When he hung up the phone, he filled us in. "They weren't able to deliver the cake today because they got stuck in traffic."

"Stuck in traffic all day? That's not possible. Maybe they should have planned it better—"

"Don't worry, I'll explain. They're dumb," Mika conceded, giving me a nod, "and didn't plan well and didn't deliver the cake in time today."

My husband sure knew how to talk me off the ledge! I listened politely while he continued. "The good news is they promise to deliver the cake between 3 pm and 6 pm tomorrow."

Everyone cheered. My dad hugged me, sweaty from our boxing match. "That's great, honey! Nothing to worry about. Now, you ready for me to knock you out again? The toilet water is swirling—you're going down!"

But I couldn't laugh at my dad's juvenile humor. I knew I should be happy that the cake delivery had worked out but I was fuming.

"Just to be sure I have this straight, after all the phone calls and extra money and going to their store to hand over said money and stressing out about the delivery, in the end they're going to deliver the cake EXACTLY WHEN I WANTED IN THE FIRST PLACE, exactly what they said WASN'T possible?"

"Um... yes."

"That's just..." I looked over at my dad, who was holding out my Wii controller, his eyes begging me to be cool. "That's just... perfect. Thank you."

Throwing a right-hook into my dad's animated face, I made two decisions. One—on this day, I would be happy that things had worked out. Then two—as soon as I had a few spare minutes—I would write a book about France and include stories like this. Something good had to come out of the insanity.

In the meantime, I had champagne.

41

Here Comes the Bride

"Aujourd'hui, il fera beau, avec beaucoup de soleil!"

My radio alarm had gone off at 9:00 and the meteorologist greeted me with the wonderful news of sunshine forecast for the entire day.

Mika got ready in about five minutes, as guys do, then headed out with the boys for beer and burgers before the ceremony.

The girls arrived one by one and the apartment soon became a flurry of make-up, hair dryers, mini sandwiches, and champagne. My voice was still hoarse and my ankle was still swollen, but I was hangover-free for my wedding day.

Well, assuming I didn't over-imbibe on the bubbly.

"Do you mind doing my hair, too?" Maid of Honor asked my step-mom. A hair stylist by trade, Marsha had offered to do everyone's hair on one condition—that she knew in advance whose hair she'd be doing so she could budget her time accordingly. This last-minute change threw her for a loop but she graciously accepted.

After putting the finishing touches on everyone's hair, Marsha had to scramble to get ready herself.

Downing the last of the champagne, I glanced at the clock. "You ladies all look lovely! Now, let's get a move on." Thanks to Maid of Honor's selfish request, we were now running late for the photo shoot in the park, but could catch up if we hurried.

We descended the five flights of stairs at a snail's pace, barely avoiding tripping over heels and dresses. How could we make up the time, particularly with my swollen ankle?

We shuffled down the street as fast as we could, Mom holding up the back of my dress to keep it from touching the grimy sidewalk. The fresh autumn breeze cooled my bare arms. And my armpits. Rushing around (and stressing out) had made me break out in a sweat.

Still, I couldn't help but bask in the awesomeness of the day. How many people can walk to their wedding? And pass such beautiful scenery on the way?

From time to time (OK, a lot) I griped about my life in Paris, but moments like this reminded me why I stayed. In the wise words of Ferris Bueller (anyone? anyone?) "if you don't stop and look around once in a while, you could miss it."

৽৹৵

Three hundred photos later, we arrived at the square in front of the church. Guests filed in as we split up the group—my mom, dad, and bridesmaids scurried behind the church with me while everyone else joined the masses inside.

"Oh no! My shoes are all dusty!" My mom was in a mild state of panic. "It must have been from the gravel paths in the park."

"That sucks, Mom, but what do you want me to do about it? I'm kind of about to get married here."

"I thought Charles mentioned some special tissues for wiping the dust off?"

"Magical Shoe Wiping Tissues? I'm not sure those exist, Mom. He probably just said 'tissues'." I was lucky if my mom's dusty shoes were the biggest problem on my wedding day but at the same time, I didn't have any tissues conveniently tucked anywhere. Crap.

"Here you go, Ellen," my dad offered, tugging a tissue out of a miniature pack in his pocket. He winked at me. "I prepared for my daughter's wedding day. I showed up on time and brought tissues. That's all I needed to do, right?"

"You did a great job, Dad."

The pipe organ struck its first notes, signaling the mother-of-the bride and the rest of the bridal party to head down the aisle.

"See you inside!" I shouted. "Guess it's just us now, Dad. The music will change when it's our turn to walk down the aisle."

"I can't believe my daughter's all grown up. What a day."

"Don't get cheesy on me. But yeah, I can hardly believe it either."

"I'm so happy for you. And Mika's great. And this trip is great. Everything is great."

Uh-oh. I recognized the "everything is great" mentality. "Dad, how much did you drink this morning?"

"Ha, don't worry honey. Only two beers. How much champagne did you have, young lady?"

"Only two glasses."

"See, we're—"

"Hold on! Is that the music?" I peeked around the corner and saw everyone standing in the pews, looking right back at me. "Oh no, Dad! The music's playing. We have to go!"

We composed ourselves, then ambled down the aisle, hoping the song wouldn't run out before we made it to the front.

"How long do you think it was playing?" I asked my dad through a smile, turning for the cameras.

"Not too long, honey," he said, smiling back while mugging for the cameras himself. "At least let's tell ourselves that, OK?"

"Deal."

ཙ❀ལ

At the front of the church, I was greeted with a pleasant surprise. Similar to the ornate chairs at the civil ceremony, two wood-carved chairs waited for us. They were practically thrones. As if I didn't feel like royalty already, with all the attention, the ancient stone church, and the fancy outfits!

It's a shame you only get one wedding. I could really get used to this.

The ceremony itself was short and sweet, which my sweaty armpits were grateful for. Père Nicolas delivered a wonderful service, with his sneakers peeking out from his officious robes.

It was perfect.

ཙ❀ལ

Once we were officially married in the eyes of God (at least I hope my comprehension of the French language got me that far), it was time for the final Wedding Week event—the reception! That's what it's all about, right?

I crossed my fingers that everything would be in place when we arrived. That the cake and flowers had been delivered, that the guests had found their way from the church to the venue, that there would be enough food and drinks for everyone.

Or at least enough champagne so that no one would know the difference.

"Welcome, Monsieur and Madame Lesage!"

The large doors swung open as we entered the Swedish Society. Many of the guests had already arrived, their smiling faces peeking around our huge flower arrangement in the foyer.

As we made our way to the Grand Salon, I noticed bouquets everywhere. "How is this possible? We only ordered the one in the entryway."

"These flowers are left over from a party for the King and Queen of Norway. We hope you don't mind we kept them. They match very well, *ja?*" Sonja asked.

As if I would mind. I wanted to make a crown out of the royal flowers and roll around in the rest of them on the floor. The King and Queen had been here! At *my* wedding venue!

"Vicki?" Mika asked. "You still here?"

"Yes! Just off in thought." The flower crown could wait. Mika slid a glass of champagne into my hand as my eyes landed on three layers of wedding cake. "It's here! The cake! It's a miracle."

"Everything came together. Thanks, sweetie, for all your organizing."

"Thank *you* for everything you did. It's not easy dealing with the French. I should know, I'm married to one."

 споле

At one point in the evening, this annoying girl kept requesting songs from the DJ and he kept turning her down. That girl was me.

"Everything OK?" Mika asked.

"Yeah, it's fine, though it'd be a lot better if this douchebag played some ABBA."

Before Mika could respond, I burst out laughing. Who cared about a silly song? Our guests were dancing, mingling, drinking. The affair had gone off without a hitch. Six years in France had prepared me for the worst, and instead I'd ended up with the perfect day.

"Now I've... had... the time of my life..." sprung from the speakers.

Ah, there we go. I set down my champagne flute. "Wanna dance?" I asked my husband.

"Of course."

Epilogue

Introducing Madame Lesage

"It's good to be back," I said to Mika, both of us out of breath from hauling our suitcases up the five flights. We'd taken a delayed honeymoon—a relaxing ten day Mediterranean cruise—but were happy to return to dry land.

Our wedding guests had been home now for months, but we still received calls and emails saying what a great time everyone had. I had dropped my last thank you note in the mail before setting sail, wanting to promptly thank our generous friends and family.

Now I was ready to settle into reality. Married life. Welcome, Madame Lesage.

My reverie screeched to a halt.

Crap. Madame Lesage. All my documents still sported my maiden name. While I was normally on top of things (remember the Wedding Welcome Packet?) I'd let myself slack on this one since I needed my passport in my maiden name for our honeymoon.

Now I had no excuse. No more procrastinating. Time to face French administration yet again and change my name on every document from utility bills to my visa.

This was going to hurt.

I pictured the work ahead of me. Appointments at the *Préfecture*, the bank, the social security office. Sending written letters with proof of name change to credit card companies, utility providers, the apartment rental agency. Photocopies. Signatures flying and ink drying.

I sighed. It could wait another day, right?

For now, I could spend time with my new husband. And hey, at least I wasn't alone. He could help me navigate the sea of paperwork we were about to set sail on.

Plus, we'd just found out we would have two more helping hands on board. Yep, the plus sign on the pregnancy test indicated that Baby Lesage, half-French, half-American, was on his way to his own life in Paris.

That bundle of joy would bring its own bundle of paperwork and bureaucracy. Dual citizenship, health care, taxes, and a slew of other things I hadn't even begun to think about.

Not to mention nine months *sans* alcohol.

I poured a sparkling water and gazed into Mika's deep brown eyes. Maybe the baby would have his eyes. Or maybe my green eyes. Either way, we had an exciting road ahead of us.

Clinking glasses, we toasted. "Here's to Paris."

See how Vicki handles motherhood in the City of Light in *Confessions of a Paris Potty Trainer*!

A Note from Vicki Lesage

Dear Reader,

Thanks for reading *Confessions of a Paris Party Girl*! The idea started out as a series of blog posts, then transformed radically into an entire book. I changed nearly every word from those original articles, but the sentiment remains the same: life in Paris was mostly wonderful but sometimes woeful, oftentimes awesome and occasionally awful, yet I wouldn't trade it for anything. Thank you for being a part of my journey.

I hope you enjoyed the book! If so, I'd love it if you left a review on Amazon.com. For every review—even just a few sentences—I receive a cupcake. OK, not really. But customer reviews encourage readers to try out new books, which is arguably better. Depending on the flavor of cupcake.

If you'd like to see where my adventure in Paris went next, check out *Confessions of a Paris Potty Trainer*! I also post updates on what I'm doing these days on my website and in my newsletters. I only send a few newsletters per year, and I send you a free ebook of *Confessions & Cocktails* when you sign up.

Thanks for reading!

À bientôt,
Vicki

P.S. Read on for a sneak peek of *Confessions of a Paris Potty Trainer*...

CATCH UP ON THE
American in Paris
BEST-SELLING SERIES

Find out about new releases and deals
by signing up for Vicki's newsletter:
https://bit.ly/lesage-news

(She'll even send you *Confessions & Cocktails* for free!)

Confessions
of a Paris
Potty Trainer

A HUMOROUS PARENTING MEMOIR

VICKI LESAGE

press

1

Safe Sex on the Beach

Perusing the chalkboard menu at the cozy Scottish pub, every drink looked good to me. Well, not the whisky. I don't need a drink that puts hair on my chest. I prefer something sweet. Or bubbly. Or both.

My husband, Mika, and I were seated at our usual spot at the bar. Mika had already ordered a beer. And our friend Anne Marie, the cheery Irish bartender with a wave of reddish hair, was giving me the eye.

"C'mon you. What's the big decision? Glass of wine like usual, yeah?"

A glass of Bordeaux isn't typical fare for a Scottish pub, except this particular bar was located in the Marais, a trendy but lovely part of Paris. Too trendy (read: expensive) for us to live in, so we lived in the less trendy (read: still expensive but at least doable) 15th *arrondissement*.

Mika and I were frequent customers of this bar, partly because we loved it and partly because Anne Marie now worked there. She'd previously been employed at the posh Swedish Society, the private club where we'd been regulars and also where we had our wedding reception.

Now just a few short months after I'd entered into marital bliss, I was pregnant with my first baby.

Hence the drink dilemma.

I've read numerous articles about French doctors being pretty lenient concerning drinking while pregnant, saying that as long as you limit it to one glass of red wine per day, it's not a big deal. However, *my* doctor didn't say that. I'm beginning to think it's an urban legend, propagated to make the French seem loose and carefree and make Americans jealous.

Articles and stereotypes aside, I had already decided I wouldn't drink during my pregnancy. Which, as a well-known party girl, was going to be difficult.

In my pre-pregnant days—in an effort to make sure my perfect-for-jeans butt still fit in said jeans even after consuming vast amounts of champagne and wine and shots and... I'll stop there since my mom is going to read this—I had formed a policy. I only allowed myself to consume caloric beverages if they contained alcohol. This meant that water, black coffee, and diet soda were OK. But no juice or non-diet soda or energy drinks or any of those other empty calorie explosions.

However, when faced with a bar menu, the only choices without alcohol have calories. Might be time to revise my policy. I was eating for two now, right? I could handle the extra calories.

The other part of the dilemma was that I hadn't told Ammo yet that I was pregnant. I had just reached the 12th week and Mika and I had jointly decided it was now safe to share the news. Our parents already knew but no one else. A Facebook post would be the easiest way to reach my friends in all corners of the world (have we really not modified that expression since we discovered the earth was round?). But then the friends I normally saw in person might be offended that's how they found out. But then again, with the fatigue of pregnancy already setting in, combined with the fact that I couldn't drink, I wasn't making the rounds with my friends as often as I used to.

And holy smokes, how long had I been sitting here thinking about this while Anne Marie was waiting for an answer?

If I wasn't careful I would turn into one of the annoying French customers who comes to a pub, takes forever to order, settles on the cheapest option, then nurses their drink all night while watching the game on TV. I wouldn't be allowed to make fun of those people if I was doing the exact same thing.

"Um, what's good that doesn't have alcohol? My stomach feels a bit..."

"OH. MY. GOD. Vicki Lesage is pregnant. Oh my god! Congratulations you two!" Anne Marie bounded out from behind the bar and embraced us in a bear hug.

I could have tried to deny it, but I had been planning on telling her anyway. "How did you know?"

"Um, when have you ever not ordered alcohol in a bar? If you were sick you would have stayed home." She had a point. "Wow. Congrats."

"Thanks," Mika chimed in, his big brown eyes creasing at the corners as he couldn't help but smile.

"I have to ask, you know, since you just got married. Accident or planned?"

I would have been shocked except Ammo always asked questions like this. "You know how organized I am! Of course this wasn't on accident, it was planned down to the minute."

"I shoulda known. And I see you're still saying 'on accident.'"

She'd corrected me several times before, to no avail. "Sorry, but 'by accident' just doesn't sound right. You either do something on purpose or on accident. You wouldn't say you did something 'by purpose.'"

Mika continued sipping his beer, glancing at the game. The subtleties of the English language were lost on my French husband. Then again, apparently they were lost on me, too.

"Anyway, your drink. Without alcohol. Are you sure you're going to be OK? Nine months without alcohol?"

"Well, I'm already three months in, so we're a third of the way there. It's rough but it's for a good cause."

"Yeah, yeah. OK, how about I make you a Safe Sex on the Beach?"

"So, a juice?" That didn't fit my no-calorie policy and it sounded terribly boring.

"It's not a juice if you call it Safe Sex on the Beach. This is as much fun as you'll be having for a while, so try to enjoy it." She winked before turning around to mix up my concoction.

As I waited for my "cocktail," I sized up the situation. I had taken forever to order, I ended up with the cheapest drink on the menu, and was probably going to nurse it all night since there's no point in chugging juice. The only thing keeping me from being a fully annoying French customer was the fact I wasn't watching the game. Oh, and the fact that I was American. But with a French husband and a half-French baby on the way, I was dangerously close.

After a few splashes from various juice bottles and vigorous shakes with a martini shaker (ah, martinis), Ammo poured my Safe Sex on the Beach into an ice-filled glass. Then she poured a shot of whisky[20] for herself.

---

[20] American and Irish readers might be thinking "Um, isn't it spelled 'whiskey'?" The answer is: yes and no. Some countries who produce the liquor spell it with an 'e,' some don't. The easiest way to remember is that countries that produce it whose name contains an 'e,' such as The United States and Ireland, spell it with an 'e.' Countries that produce it whose name does not contain an 'e,' such as Scotland, Canada, and Japan, spell it without the 'e.' As an American in France talking about the liquor being served in a Scottish pub, I could probably get away with either spelling, but decided to go with the Scottish way since Ammo was drinking Scotch whisky. Whew! After all that, I might need a shot of whisky after all.

"Cheers to my old, married, knocked-up friend. Congrats."

Ammo, Mika, and I clinked glasses.

"Cheers."

Find out what happens next... pick up *Confessions of a Paris Potty Trainer* today!

About the Author

Vicki lived in Paris for 11 years, where she met her husband, Mika, and had two kids, Leo and Stella. After realizing that a one-bedroom Parisian apartment was too small for the four of them, they moved to Vicki's hometown of St. Louis and have been enjoying all the extra space ever since. Vicki still misses croissants and baguettes and stinky cheese, though.

Catch up on the latest from Vicki:
Website: VickiLesage.com
Newsletter: https://bit.ly/lesage-news
Facebook: https://www.facebook.com/vickilesagewriter

And you can always drop Vicki a line at vicki@vickilesage.com. Mail from readers is the best part of her day. Unless the kids actually let her sleep in for once, in which case she'll get to your email momentarily!

Acknowledgements

Many thanks to Ellen Meyer, also known as Mom, who gave me the push needed to transform years of blogging into an actual book. I wouldn't have done it without her promise to edit, re-edit, and format the whole thing for me. She spent countless hours making this a better book and supported me the entire way.

Huge thanks to Marie Vareille, fellow author and meticulous editor, who read the book more times than I can count and provided invaluable feedback. And English is her second language!

Special thanks to my other wonderful friends who read the book and provided insightful feedback: Anne Marie Higgins, who you all know and love by now; Erika Gennari, who appears under a pseudonym to protect the innocent; Erin Lizzo, who was my partner in crime on my first trip to Europe, making me fall in love with the continent; and Bastien Jaillot, a French colleague who actually works, but of course still found time to read my book and find plenty of critiques.

I'd also like to thank Clara Vidal for spicing up my cover design, adding that perfect French touch, and Damien Croisot for polishing up my author photo. If only he could make my skin look that good in real life!

I want to thank my husband, Mickaël Lesage, for his unwavering support and encouragement. He's not always objective but sometimes you just need someone who loves your work unconditionally to help you get through the project. And I'd like to thank Leonardo, who was smaller than a poppy seed at the end of this book but has grown into a beautiful baby boy, who is usually patient when Mommy just needs to write one last sentence.

Made in the USA
Lexington, KY
07 November 2018